THE CRIME WRITER'S SOURCEBOOK

(Using True Crime in Fiction)

Other Allison & Busby Writers' Guides

THE
CRIME WRITER'S
SOURCEBOOK

(Using True Crime in Fiction)

Douglas Wynn

a&b

First published in Great Britain in 2000 by
Allison & Busby Ltd
114 New Cavendish Street
London W1M 7FD
http://www.allisonandbusby.ltd.uk

A catalogue record for this book is available from
the British Library.

ISBN 0 7490 0461 4

Typeset by DAG Publications Ltd, London.
Printed and bound in Great Britain by
Biddles Ltd, Guildford.

ACKNOWLEDGEMENTS

I must thank Gordon Wells for his invaluable help in pulling together my somewhat disparate ideas of what this book should be like, in refusing to give up on me and ensuring that it came to a happy conclusion. Thanks also go to Martin Duckworth for helpful discussions on forensic science aspects and to Roger Forsdyke, as ever, for advice on police matters, but I should emphasise that any mistakes are mine and mine alone. I am grateful to Gregg Manning for permission to quote from his website. I should also like to thank Martin Edwards and all my friends at the Northern Chapter of the Crime Writers Association whose assistance and comments have helped in the construction and the detail of the work.

As always, to Rosemary, without whose encouragement and support none of my writing would ever see the light of day, my thanks and love.

CONTENTS

7

CONTENTS

1

INTRODUCTION AND SEARCHING
FOR SOURCE MATERIAL

Have you ever thought that you would like to write a crime novel, but couldn't think of a really good idea? Or are you on your fifth or sixth novel and finding that new and fresh twists are getting harder to come by? Perhaps you have started but are finding that the plot is turning out to be just a little bit hackneyed, and you are losing interest in your characters? Worry no more! Turn to true crime for inspiration and your troubles will be over.

You may have already felt that some of those sensational murder cases of which our newspapers are so full these days might be suitable for adaptation into a novel, but perhaps you haven't come across one that sparked your interest. Or possibly you may have felt that some of the protagonists sound as if they might be turned into interesting fictional characters, but you didn't know enough about them to be able to tell.

This book is an attempt to present some intriguing and exciting cases that hopefully will help to spark off some ideas and some characters which will help to stimulate your imagination. Most of the cases are fairly recent, giving an up-to-date picture of the crime scene, but some are not. Take the Conrad case, for example …

In a working-class suburb of Berlin in 1881, Conrad, the driver of a horse and cart, stopped a policeman and complained that he couldn't get into his apartment. When the door was eventually forced it was found to be bolted on the inside and Conrad's wife was hanging by the neck from a hook in the ceiling. Inside a cupboard were the carter's five small children. They had all been strangled and hung from coat hooks. Conrad said that they were desperately short of money and he supposed that his wife had strangled the children and then committed suicide. But the police were suspicious since, although the bodies were all nearly skeletons, the husband himself was well nourished. It was then found that he had a girlfriend upon whom he lavished a considerable amount of money.

But if he had killed his wife and family, how had he done it inside a locked room to which there was no access except through the door? The police discovered that Conrad was a great reader and one of his books was a translation of an English crime novel, *Nena Sahib* by John Radcliffe. This featured a 'locked room' murder in which a tiny hole had been bored in the door near the bolt which had then been worked home from the outside by a piece of wire. It was found, examining Conrad's door, that this is exactly what he had done, but he had used woven horse hair instead of wire.

This clearly was a case of life imitating art. But it is much more common to find things the other way round; a real-life murder case used as the basis of a crime novel. In fact most of the well-known murder cases of the last two hundred years have been used as the starting point in the construction of crime stories, some of them many times over.

The Crippen case is a good example. Dr Hawley Harvey Crippen was an American who poisoned his wife, whose stage name was Belle Elmore, with hyoscine in London early in 1910, cut up the body and buried parts of it under the cellar floor. He would probably have got away with it except that he panicked and boarded a ship for Canada with his mistress Ethel le Neve. But the captain of the SS *Montrose* thought there was something suspicious about Ethel (who was dressed as a boy) and radioed London. Chief Inspector Dew, who was in charge of the case, boarded a faster ship and the pair were arrested as the SS *Montrose* docked. This was the first time, incidentally, that radio had been used in a murder case. Although le Neve was acquitted, Crippen was convicted of murder and hanged.

There have been a dozen novels, plays or films based on this case. *Henbane*, a novel first published in 1934 and written by Catherine Meadows, is about a Dr Moon and his wife Flora, whom he hates, and his secretary Maria with whom he is in love. The story follows closely the facts of the real case, but gives the writer's own interpretation of the motives of the doctor and his mistress. The other extreme is Peter Lovesey's novel *The False Inspector Dew*, which won the Crime Writers' Association Gold Dagger award for the best crime novel of 1982, and developed when the author wondered what might have happened had Crippen, instead of murdering his wife in Hilldrop Crescent, London, taken her on the ship with the idea of murdering her there. But the plot of this delightful story has so many twists and turns that if there weren't references in it to the Crippen case even a reader well acquainted with the murder would have difficulty in realising the source of the plot.

But although nearly every major crime in the last hundred years or so has been pressed into the service of story-telling it doesn't mean that the source has all but dried up. There is always a new interpretation which can be placed on the facts. Different twists can be inserted, or the writer, like Peter Lovesey, can use the case merely to spark off ideas which when developed might lead to a totally different story. In addition there are crimes being committed every day and many of them can and no doubt will be used as the basis of a piece of fiction. A recent one concerned Albert Walker, a fugitive Canadian businessman who was convicted of taking another man's identity and then murdering him. At least two books are already being written about the case, although they will probably be non-fiction works, and three films are in the pipeline, which will very likely have some element of fiction in them. Indeed one film director has said that he finds the story irresistible and the complexity of Walker's character and his secret lives, he expects, will attract the interest of several prominent actors.

This then is the purpose of the book. It is to supply interesting and intriguing true stories which might spark the imaginations of writers. Not to tell writers how to construct plots or develop characters. There are other books which give this sort of information. This one is merely there to help the creative process get started.

In each story the facts of the crime are related and a certain amount of technical detail is incorporated, such as the mechanism by which the crime was solved. General technical details have been avoided as these can be obtained from the *Crime Writer's Handbook* by Douglas Wynn, also published by Allison & Busby. But some aspects of forensic science and occasionally scientific details, or those associated with the police or law, have been included if they do not appear in the *Handbook*.

But supposing that the account of a crime merely whets your appetite and you would like to know more about the case? Well, included at the end of each story are one or two references – a book or article on the case, or newspapers that had a good coverage, so you can delve further if you wish. And if you would like to go still further, or would like to read some more true crime to see if you can find some intriguing cases for yourself, the next section tells you how to get hold of information about real-life crimes, where to go to for material and what resources are available.

Books and Magazines on True Crime

Most of the larger book shops today have sections labelled True Crime, usually near if not next to the Crime Fiction section. Libraries have collections that are classified usually under the Dewey Decimal System, which will be discussed later. Since books have been written about true crimes from well before the last century there is a substantial second-hand market in the subject and a browse through almost any second-hand bookshop will turn up a few of the genre. Occasionally these books can be found at anti-quarian book fairs and there are places such as Hay-on-Wye in Powys, Wales, which have a large number of second-hand book-shops in the town.

True Crime books can be put into a number of quite definite cate-gories. The first is the encyclopedia-type book, which has lots of short entries, for example a series of cases, or a series of murderers. This type of book is very good for obtaining an initial idea. Some exam-ples of all categories are listed in the Bibliography.

But whereas this kind of book is useful for ideas, you might need possibly a little more information on a particular case, simply to see if it is worth investigating further. The second type of book, therefore, describes a smaller collection of cases, possibly ten to twenty, but giving a lot more detail on each one. This second category itself comes under a number of headings.

The first is the themed book: collections of articles linked by a common theme, for example, murders associated with the medical profession, or killings for gain. Then there is the geographical book, which contains cases from a particular area of the country. Another type is the 'Rough Justice' kind of collection, which presents cases in which it is claimed someone has been unjustly convicted. Then again there are collections of crimes which concentrate more on forensic science and present cases that have been solved by this means.

The third category is the one-case-per-book. These books give a geat deal of information about a particular crime and often supply biographies of the participants as well. This can often spark off the interest of a writer trying to develop a fictional character. Care must be taken, of course, not to base a character directly on a real person, and to be on the safe side it is better to take characteristics from several real people rather than one.

There are a large number of one-case-per-book works. In fact this category is easily the largest. The American writers are particularly skilful at this sort of book and most are well researched and contain extensive biographies of all the leading players. And it seems that every well-known American murder and major crime has had at least one non-fiction book written about it. There are also some very good accounts from British writers and again most of the major cases of this country have had at least one book written about them. Home grown writers also seem to go in for more of the 'Rough Justice' type of book than the Americans do and writers like Ludovic Kennedy and Paul Foot have drawn attention to some notable miscarriages of justice.

Another large group comprises biographies and autobiographies, reminiscences and memoirs. These can be presented by detectives (police and private), barristers, solicitors and judges, forensic scientists, pathologists, psychologists and psychiatrists and even ex-employees of the FBI, particularly those who have been associated with the offender profiling programmes. This type of book often gives the viewpoint of an actual participant in a case and can be very useful for getting the 'inside' information about a particular crime. But do remember to check all facts obtained in this type of book if possible with another source, since on occasion the memories of experts have proved to be unreliable.

There are books which contain descriptions, often quite detailed, of particular trials, or collection of trials. Examples of these are again listed in the Bibliography. These are well worthwhile studying since quite often the reported proceedings of a trial is the only public information which one can obtain about a case, unless one of the participants has written about it or been interviewed and the interview published in a book or elsewhere. This also applies to newspaper accounts, which will be mentioned later.

Magazines

A list of magazines, both British and overseas, publishing true crime is given in the Bibliography. Many of these magazines are well illustrated and it is sometimes helpful to have actual pictures of the people involved in a crime and of the locations of the crimes. Illustrations can spark off ideas or give a feeling or an atmosphere that can assist in the writing of a crime story.

Newspapers

Newspapers are one of the best sources of information on crimes. The national dailies, such as *The Times*, the *Telegraph*, and the tabloids, usually give good coverage to the more sensational cases; such as murders and the smashing of drug rings, but the place to really find information is the local paper. Not necessarily the local paper of the town where the trial took place, but in the local paper of the area where the accused actually lived. I once researched a murder which occurred in rural Lincolnshire, but could find little about it in the local Lincoln paper, where the trial took place, but there was plenty about it in the newspaper serving the locality of the crime. In the 1920s and 1930s, when newsprint was cheap, local papers were much bigger than they are today and had many more pages. And a report of a trial would almost be a transcript of the proceedings.

In addition, a coroner's jury sits in judgement on a suspicious death, charged with determining how, when and where the death occurred and until 1978 it was also their duty to say who was to be charged. This meant that in some cases the coroner's court could become a trial *en petit* which would be reported extensively in the local paper. Then would come the committal proceedings, which used to be a lot more lengthy than they are today, with the prosecution setting out their case in almost as much detail as in the trial itself. This might be followed in due course by the actual trial. So, effectively you might get the case reported, in great detail, three times in the local newspaper.

The local library will often have back issues of the local newspapers which you can look at, or, failing that, a trip to the British Library Newspaper Library, Colindale Avenue, London NW9 5HE (tel: 020 7323 7353) – opposite Colindale Underground station – would be worthwhile. This library keeps copies of all British newspapers, both local and national, back to about the eighteenth century. Overseas newspapers in English are also stored and you can consult, for example: Australian, New Zealand, South African, and many American and Canadian local newspapers. A reader's ticket is necessary but this can be obtained on the day of your visit.

Public Record Office

The Public Record Office (Ruskin Avenue, Kew, Surrey TW9 4DU, (tel: 020 8392 5200, fax: 020 8392 5286, e-mail: enquiry@pro.gov.uk, website: http://www.pro.gov.uk/) has assizes records for England and Wales. Up till 1733, though, they were mostly written in Latin and heavily abbreviated. To find a case you will usually have to know the county or assize circuit and the approximate date of the assize sitting. But if you write to or phone the PRO they will send you a useful leaflet on assize records which gives the assize circuits and other useful information. The assize sessions were abolished in 1971 and replaced by crown courts. But it is as well to remember that you are not entitled to see material that is less than thirty years old in the public records.

Records of quarter sessions, courts which used to try less serious cases than assizes, are held in County Record Offices or Regional Archives, a list of which, together with addresses, is given in *Research for Writers* by Ann Hoffman, an indispensable book for all writers that covers many aspects of research on all kinds of subjects.

Libraries

Most British libraries use the Dewey Decimal System, which seeks to classify knowledge into ten classes: 000 for General Works, to 900 for Geography, Biography and History. True Crime comes under 300 (Social Sciences) and can be found under 340–49 (Law), 350–59 and also under 360–65 (Social Problems). The reason for the placing of books in a number of categories comes from the difficulty of defining True Crime. Does a book of trials, for example, come under Law or another heading? So, when searching a library, look under a number of designations. The reminiscences of an eminent judge or advocate might easily come under Biography.

If you want a particular book, and know the title and author, yet cannot find it on the shelves, you can consult the library staff. They will be able to consult a database and tell you if the book is in the hands of another borrower or can be obtained from another library.

Police

Some police forces are very helpful to writers trying to research a case, others are not quite so accommodating. The best thing to do is to write to the press officer or the public relations department of the force concerned, put your query and ask for help. The address can be obtained from the *Police and Constabulary Almanac*, published yearly by R. Hazell and Co., P.O. Box 39, Henley-on-Thames, Oxfordshire R99 5UA, which should be available in your local library. If the case is an old one, you might be able to contact a retired policeman who worked on the case and get some personal reminiscences.

Visiting the Scene of the Crime

Obviously, one would not visit the scene of a recent crime, especially if the police are still there! But visiting the scene after you have made a study of the case can be very profitable. You can absorb atmosphere (often important for a fiction writer) and sometimes understand more clearly the the mechanics of a crime.

I once researched a murder which took place in 1947 near the Standedge Pass on the A62 road between Huddersfield and Oldham. The murderer, a young man called John Gartside, had no previous convictions for violence, but, at their home, he inexplicably shot and killed a middle-aged couple who lived not far from him, whom he didn't even know. But after studying the case and visiting the location the reason soon became obvious.

Gartside lived with his parents in a large house on the main road. From the windows he could easily see the couple's house further up the steep hillside behind and would notice them go out in their car. He decided to burgle their house and, being a member of a gun club, took a rifle and a pistol with him, possibly to bolster his confidence. When they returned unexpectedly and caught him in their house it is easy to speculate that he first tried to hold them up with his guns, but then shot them both, possibly in a panic. He subsequently buried their bodies up on the moor. He was convicted and hanged for the double murder.

Visiting Courts

Many of the bigger towns these days have crown courts which handle serious cases involving robbery with violence, rape and even murder. All these courts have public galleries, although they may not be very big, where it is possible to sit and listen to a case in progress. This helps the writer to learn about court procedure and the way evidence is presented. And, conditioned as we are to seeing television drama court scenes played by actors, it is salutary to see how ordinary but real people cope with what is for most an extremely stressful and sometimes excruciatingly embarrassing situation. And if nothing else it might help a writer to pen some authentic court scenes.

The Internet

If you have a PC which can connect to the Internet there is a vast amount of material literally at your fingertips. Because, however, websites change frequently and what you can find on the Internet depends to a certain extent on the web browser and search engine you use, I will try to give you only my own experience.

Using my web browser AOL Netfind, typing in the word 'Crime' and asking the browser to search 'The Whole Web', I recently (March 1999) found 268,919 pages. Of course this did include sites with a very tenuous connection to crime. For example, one advertised: 'the sights, sounds, and smells of a medieval village surround you as you walk down the street … while knights and their pages patrol the streets looking for troublemakers.' But on the other hand there were sites where you could buy crime books, read articles about the Mafia, or view pictures from, it was claimed, actual police files.

INTRODUCTION

If I narrowed the search down to 'True Crime', then the browser came up with only 59,418 pages. Again there were a great many sites to help search for True Crime books, but there were also plenty of sites with articles on the subject. An example taken at random is 'Famous Murders through history compiled by Gregg Manning' (website address http://grape.orangenet.co.uk/~greggman/). The Table of Contents includes 'Famous Hangmen and notable executions', 'Female Serial Killers', 'Films based on true stories', 'Judges and Counsel', 'Methods or weapons used by the murderer on the victim', 'Motive for committing the murder', 'Murder Cases – Male', 'Complete cases', 'Murder cases – Female', 'Murder Cases – Partnerships', 'Reference Material', 'Rogues' Gallery', 'Sentence as passed by the court', 'Victim of the crime', 'Prison where the criminal was held', 'Pathologists', 'Crimes and Legal Terms'. The components of each chapter are usually short pieces, 200 to 300 words, and in total this website would equal in terms of amount of material a fair-sized encyclopaedia in book form. This at a fraction of the cost of the book. And of course if you want it in permanent form you can always print it out after downloading it.

2

THE MURDEROUS MALE – FEMALE VICTIMS

Love, Jealousy or Hate

The Eve Howells Case

August 31st 1995 was a Thursday and that night 47-year-old David Howells played a darts match at his local pub in Huddersfield. His two sons, Glenn, who was 15, and John, 14, found their mother battered to death in the living room of their bungalow. Glenn told the police that earlier in the evening his brother John had given his mother Eve, who was a year older than her husband, a pedicure as he usually did on a Thursday night. Then she had told them to take the dog for a walk. When they returned she ordered them to go out again as they hadn't given the dog sufficient exercise. He took the dog while his brother rode off on his bike. When Glenn returned he found his mother sprawled across a bean bag in the blood-spattered room. She had received a dozen severe injuries to her head. Furniture was over-turned in the room and it appeared to be an attempted burglary that had got out of hand.

But the police were suspicious from the start. Mrs Howells had no defence wounds on her hands or arms as might have been expected if she had been attacked by a burglar. In fact, from the blood spattering pattern it looked as she had been struck from behind while she was sitting on the bean bag writing letters, as apparently she often did. In addition there was a recent bloodstain underneath an overturned chair, which indicated it had been tipped over after the attack.

The next day the police insisted that both boys and their father make a formal identification of the body. Glenn seemed quite unconcerned over the ordeal and only broke down crying when he saw the other two in tears. And later he was seen winking at his younger brother. This was certainly suspicious, but the police needed more than that.

They sent all the boys' and their father's clothes, towels and bed linen for forensic examination. The results were illuminating. A small amount of blood was found on a pair of Glenn Howells's socks and on a towel and a flannel. DNA testing identified it as belonging to Eve Howells. And some small spots of blood on a jacket of John's also came from his mother.

The teenagers were arrested three weeks after the murder. There was plenty of motive. Mrs Howells, who had an eating disorder and weighed only six stone when she died, had ruled her family with a rod of iron. She dominated them, ran the finances and had recently closed a joint account with her husband to set up two separate ones. She put £51,000 in her account and £100 in her husband's. For years she had apparently terrorised her children, continually screaming abuse at them, according to her neighbours, and beating them frequently. She would often threaten to burn their favourite cuddly toys. She kept a lock on the fridge and regulated everything the family ate. An intelligent woman, with a degree in History, she was a local school teacher. Yet she was known to the pupils as 'Evil Howells', and had a reputation as a vindictive disciplinarian who had received many complaints both from pupils and parents.

The boys could well be guilty, but what about the father? Was he involved? He had the perfect alibi, but had he set it up and convinced the boys to kill their mother, or was he as shocked and surprised by what had happened as he claimed? Then the police discovered that although Eve Howells had had an affair with a family friend for twelve years, Howells himself had only found out about it recently. He also stood to come into £150,000 on his wife's death.

The police decided on a bold move. They would bug the cells where the boys were held when their father came to visit them. But to do this Detective Superintendent Gary Haigh, who was in charge of the case, had to observe Home Office guidelines. He had to get permission first from his force's Assistant Chief Constable who had to satisfy himself that four criteria were met. Firstly, that the investigation involved serious crime; then that normal investigation methods had been tried and failed; that there was a good reason to believe that use of the equipment would be likely to lead to an arrest and conviction; and finally that the use of the equipment was feasible. All these were judged to have been met and a visiting room at the cells was wired up before Howells met his sons there.

The ruse was spectacularly successful. Howells was heard to say: 'We have just got to bluff it out. If you two break, I'm in as well, so we've got to stick together.' Sometime later he said: 'You two are not saying you have done it. They have got to prove it.' Glenn Howells was heard to say to his father: 'You said we were going to have a good life.' 'Yes, we are,' replied his father. 'I promise you I will wait for you. We'll have a new life together with plenty of money.'

Howells was arrested, but still he couldn't keep his mouth shut. He told a cellmate he had planned the murder and chosen Glenn to do it because he was bigger. Later the younger of the boys, John, broke down in custody and confessed the whole thing. He said the murder had been planned by the three of them. In fact they had discussed getting rid of their mother for a long time and the previous year on holiday had planned to push her off a balcony at a hotel, but the plan failed because she had a ground floor room. John's job after the murder was to get rid of the bloodstained clothes and the hammer that Glenn had used to batter his mother to death. The younger boy took the police to a canal in Wakefield where the weapon was subsequently recovered.

Just before the trial Glenn confessed too and pleaded guilty to manslaughter on the grounds of provocation. But at the trial at Leeds Crown Court in January 1997 this plea was not accepted and all three were charged with murder. The jury of seven men and five women deliberated for several hours before bringing in a verdict of guilty against all three. Mr Justice Alliott then made the most unusual request, before he passed sentence, of asking Howells and his sons what really happened. But they all stuck to their original stories. The judge sentenced David Howells to life imprisonment, after saying: 'You suborned your sons into doing what they did.' The two boys, because they were juveniles, were ordered to be detained during Her Majesty's pleasure.

It was afterwards disclosed that the Lord Chief Justice, after receiving advice from the trial judge on the minimum sentence to be served by both youths for 'retribution and deterrence', had recommended to the Home Secretary that John Howells should serve seven years and Glenn ten. David Howells is understood not to have been told what minimum sentence he must serve.

References
The Times
The Huddersfield Daily Examiner

Money

The Jeremy Bamber Case

Cases of grown-up children who kill their parents are thankfully rare, but not unknown. There was the murder of Elizabeth and Nicholas Newall in Jersey by their sons Roderick and Mark in 1987, and the Menendez brothers who shot their wealthy California parents in 1989. And one must not forget Lizzie Borden, accused in 1892 of killing her father and stepmother with an axe in Fall River, Massachusetts, USA. A very similar case to the Bamber murders was that of Ronald De Feo who shot his father and mother, two sisters and two brothers to death in their house in Amityville, Long Island, in 1974. The house which was later claimed to be haunted became the subject of a best-selling book and a film, *The Amityville Horror*.

What possesses grown-up children like these to submit what you would think would be their nearest and dearest to the ultimate crime? There are obviously many reasons and many theories, but in the case of the more affluent families, like the Newalls and the Menendez family, one motive seems to come to the fore. This is money, or the possibility of inheriting large sums of money.

This certainly appeared to be the situation with Jeremy Bamber. He was adopted at the age of three months by Nevill Bamber, a wealthy landowner and farmer, and his wife June. They lived at White

House Farm on the outskirts of the small village of Tolleshunt D'Arcy, fifteen miles from Chelmsford in Essex. Nevill was an important man locally, serving as a magistrate and his wife was a pillar of the local church.

Jeremy was sent to a private prep school in Essex and then to Gresham's, an expensive boarding school in Norfolk. Apparently he deeply resented being sent away to school and his academic record there was only mediocre. People who knew him at this time said he was rather quiet and introspective, yet could be abrasive and arrogant, and he relentlessly teased younger boys. Academically he picked up a bit at Colchester College where he obtained seven O-levels. Then he spent a year in Australia and New Zealand. He was being groomed by his parents to take over the farm and when he arrived back in England he was made farm manager. His parents bought him a cottage in the nearby village of Goldhanger and gave him a company car. But instead of being grateful he seemed to resent his foster parents, particularly his foster mother, and far from settling down to a quiet life on the farm he much prefered fast cars and even faster women.

But if Jeremy appeared a bit of an oddball, his sister Sheila was much worse. She too had been adopted by the Bambers when she was a baby and was four years older than Jeremy. But she had been expelled from schools in Norwich and Eastbourne and had noticeably erratic behaviour. A very pretty girl, she had begun a promising career as a model, but turned out to be too mentally unstable to obtain regular work. At the time of the murders she was twenty-seven. She was estranged from her husband and following a nervous breakdown was staying at White House Farm with her six-year-old twin sons.

In the early hours of Wednesday, August 7th 1985, Jeremy Bamber called the Chelmsford police station to report that he was at home in Goldhanger and his father had just called him to say that his sister had gone crazy with a gun. There had been the sound of a report and the line had gone dead and when he tried to redial he got the engaged signal. The police raced to White House Farm, followed by Jeremy, and after waiting several hours, because they feared an armed person might be roaming the house, eventually broke in. They found

Nevill on the floor beside the telephone, the receiver of which was hanging down, battered and shot through the head. June was in her bedroom. She had also been attacked and shot dead. The dead bodies of the twins were still in their beds. They too had been shot. Sheila was lying near Mrs Bamber's bedroom window. She had bullet wounds in the throat and also in the head, and a .22 rifle lay across her body.

Ballistics showed that the rifle was the one which had killed all the victims and the police were soon convinced that Sheila had murdered her family and then committed suicide. But Nevill and June's nephew David Boutflour and his sister Mrs Ann Eaton were not so sure. They realised that there were holes in Jeremy's story. If the telephone was found off its rest it was very unlikely that the line would have gone dead as he said. Several days after the murder they made a search of the house and found a silencer for a rifle at the back of a gun cupboard. It had blood on it and also a grey hair which might have been Nevill's. In addition, measurements showed that the rifle with the silencer fitted would have been too long for Sheila, who had quite short arms, for her to have held it underneath her chin to shoot herself in the head. The pathology report later confirmed that the shot to the head which killed her could not have been self-inflicted.

Eventually Julie Mugford, who had been Jeremy's girlfriend, went to the police to report that he had been talking about killing his family to inherit the estate for months and had even killed rats with his bare hands to steel himself for the attack.

The trial of Jeremy Bamber took place at Chelmsford Crown Court in October 1986. He was convicted of the five murders and sentenced to five concurrent life sentences with the recommendation that he should not be released for twenty-five years. Several appeals have since been made on his behalf, but so far he remains in jail.

References

In Search of the Rainbow's End by Colin Caffell, Hodder & Stoughton, 1994

Murder in Mind, 6, Marshal Cavendish, 1998

The Times
Daily Mail
Chelmsford and South Woodham Weekly News

Sexual Gratification

The Edwin Hopkins Case

Fifteen-year-old Naomi Smith lived on the Betts Hall Estate in the former mining village of Ansley Common, close to Nuneaton. On Thursday, September 14th 1995, she left her home at about 9.45 p.m. to post a letter for her mother. Since the post box was only two hundred yards away, when she still hadn't returned after a considerable time her mother became worried. Her husband phoned to see if Naomi had gone to see her best friend Emma Jones, and finding she hadn't, he left in his car to search for his daughter. He picked up Emma and she suggested they look in the recreation ground, locally known as 'the rec', just behind the houses in the village.

He drove up an entry between two houses and Emma got out and rushed ahead to the rec, while he illuminated the area with his headlights. They both saw a white shape on the ground beneath one of the children's swings. Emma, who was in front, raced up to it, then ran back screaming and Brian Smith went on alone to see the body of his daughter.

She had been brutally sexually attacked. Her jeans were pulled down, her legs splayed wide and her throat had been slashed. The post mortem showed that one of her breasts had been savagely bitten and a large object had been forced into her vagina causing massive internal injuries. Thankfully it looked as if that had been done after her death.

The police began a meticulous search of the recreation ground and the surrounding area. They were looking for the knife which had been used to slash the girl and the object, possibly a bottle, which had been involved in the mutilation. But they found neither. Nor did they find anything that might point them in the direction of the killer. The rec was used extensively, during the day by children and by adults

26

walking their dogs, and at night by teenagers meeting their friends. It had also been the scene of gang fights in the past.

Detective Superintendent Tony Bayliss, who was leading the investigation, appealed to the public for anyone who had any information whatsoever to come forward. A young girl did so and she said that she had been standing at her parents' bedroom window on the night of the murder and had seen Naomi, whom she recognised by her light coloured bomber-style jacket, go to the post box. Naomi posted her letter then started for home. But she stopped, looked up and down the road and then retraced her steps, going on past the post box this time. She paused at the entrance to an alleyway which led behind the houses to the recreation ground. Then she turned and went into the unlit alleyway.

Part of this was soon explained. Naomi's mother said that her daughter had wanted her friend Emma to stay the night and Mrs Smith had told Naomi to look up the road when she went to the post box to see if Emma's father's car was parked at her sister's house so they could ask him. But why should Naomi sneak off up the alleyway? Did she have a date to meet a boyfriend? It seemed unlikely, since she had left her home door unlocked when she left and her regular boyfriend had an alibi for that evening and night.

The police seemed to be at an impasse. They were convinced that a great many people knew more than they were saying, but they were confronted with a wall of silence. They called in forensic psychiatrist Tony Britton. He reviewed all the evidence, went to the scene of the crime and interviewed Emma Jones in depth. He soon became convinced that Naomi would not have gone into that dark alleyway with someone she did not know. According to Emma, Naomi liked older men rather than teenagers, so Britton told the police they should be looking for an offender between his teens and mid-twenties. He would live probably no more than a quarter of a mile from the scene of the crime and would know the area, including the rec in the dark, very well. They should look for someone who could become very angry and who might have been in trouble with the police before for minor sexual offences.

Then the police had a breakthrough. Swabbings of the area around the bite on Naomi's left breast had been sent to a laboratory to see if scientists could get a DNA profile from the saliva left in the wound. Eventually they were successful. But Detective Superintendent Bayliss still had a problem. He would have liked to run a mass screening operation, taking mouth swabs from all men between 14 and 40 who lived within half a mile radius of the murder scene, to see if their saliva DNA matched that on the murder victim. This would however be prohibitively expensive. But using the psychological profile and a computer system known as WATSON he was able to narrow the search down to a much smaller group. These were tested and a match found almost immediately. He was Edwin Douglas Hopkins, 19, who lived in Ansley Common, very close to the rec. And police files revealed that a local teenage girl had alleged, two years before, that Hopkins had indecently assaulted her in the fields behind the recreation ground.

He was brought to trial at Birmingham Crown Court on January 22nd 1997. A forensic odontologist showed that there was a match between Hopkins's teeth and the marks made in the bite to Naomi's left breast. The accused's sister also gave evidence that he had been at her house on the evening of the crime, drinking and playing Trivial Pursuit until 9.30 p.m., when he had left on his bike to buy lager and crisps at an off-licence. She had expected him back within half an hour, but he had arrived much later and when he did he was wearing fresh clothes. The police revealed also that he was obsessed with knives and had a collection of Rambo-style weapons, including a machete, hung on his bedroom wall and he was known to carry knives with him. The jury returned a verdict of guilty and Mr Justice Tucker sentenced him to custody for life.

References
Paul Britton, *The Jigsaw Man*, Bantam Press, 1997
The Times

The Michael Brookes Case

This amazing case illustrates several important points: sexual gratification of a most violent kind, the long and often frustrating struggle of ordinary people for justice and then the significant issue of whether justice can be done after such a blaze of publicity,

Michael Brookes had a history of bizarre sexual behaviour. A witness, Roland Cooper, stated that when Brookes was a young man and courting Cooper's daughter, several times he caught Brookes opening his wife's fashion catalogues to the underwear pages and stabbing at the images with a knife. At the time of the murder Brookes was living with his stepson Fitzroy (usually called Roy) in the Sinfin suburb of Derby. He was also the boy's constant companion and a considerable influence upon the young man, who was only fifteen. In the lad's presence he also repeated his habit of stabbing pictures of women cut from magazines. He was also, according to Roy, an admirer of Jack the Ripper and whenever they went out he would leer at young women they saw and fantasise about stabbing them.

Lynn Siddons was sixteen and lived with her grandmother Florence only a few doors away from the Brookeses. On April 3rd 1978 she went out shopping, but did not return. Her grandmother became very worried and contacted all her friends, one of whom was Roy Brookes. He said that he had seen Lynn earlier in the day, but that they had parted and he hadn't seen her since. Six days later her body was found in bushes beside the Trent and Mersey Canal, a popular place for walkers in the Sinfin area. She had been strangled and had received forty-three stab wounds.

Roy Brookes was an obvious suspect and was questioned at a police station. Because he was a juvenile the police summoned a responsible adult to be with him during the questioning. This was Michael Brookes who spent a considerable time alone with the boy. Eventually Roy confessed to murdering Lynn. He said that she had made sexual advances to him and he had stabbed her to death.

But while awaiting trial in Leicester Prison he was interviewed by a psychiatrist and to him he told a different story. When he went for trial at the Crown Court in Nottingham in November 1978 his defence was that Michael Brookes had talked to him the day before the murder about wanting to stab Lynn. The next day he had told Roy to lure Lynn away and together the two youngsters had walked across fields towards the canal. Michael Brookes followed and when they came to some bushes, jumped on Lynn from behind and held her arms and covered her mouth. He then ordered Roy to stab her and the young man, who was afraid of his stepfather, made a few reluctant jabs at her. But Michael seized the knife and continued to stab the young girl, then pulled her to the canal bank and after immersing her head in the water hid the now dead body in some bushes.

Plainly the judge believed the young man, since he summed up in his favour, and the jury were also convinced because after retiring for only sixty minutes they brought in a verdict of not guilty. But although everyone in the courtroom must have believed that Michael Brookes was responsible for the murder, he was not charged.

This infuriated members of the Siddons family. They organised a march of protest through the centre of Derby and collected a petition containing many thousands of signatures, but nothing was done. A campaign against the Brookeses began, with posters being put up outside their house and bricks thrown through their windows. They moved house, but the intimidation continued. At one stage Michael Brookes's wife told a solicitor that he had confessed the murder to her, but then she retracted the statement and the evidence against Brookes was again reduced. Cynthia Siddons, Lynn's aunt, is said to have driven a car at Michael and his wife, but she missed and was fined £100 for reckless driving.

Eventually the Brookes family moved to Peterborough and adopted new identities. Then in April 1981 Paul Foot, feature writer for the *Daily Mirror*, who subsequently successfully campaigned on behalf of the Bridgwater Four and Colin Wallace, became interested in the case. He wrote articles in support of the Siddons family in which he pointed to Michael Brookes as the killer – a risky action which could have resulted in Foot and the *Daily Mirror* being sued for libel.

In 1985 Florence Siddons, Lynn's grandmother, made an official complaint against the Derbyshire police. This was investigated by the Merseyside police, who suggested that the Lynn Siddons case be reopened, but the recommendation was rejected by the Derbyshire force.

Paul Foot put the Siddons family in touch with Jane Deighton, a civil rights lawyer, and she suggested that Michael Brookes should be sued in the civil courts for battery, loss of expectation of life (Lynn's) and loss of earnings. The Law Society agreed to contribute towards the funding of the civil suit, since the Siddons family could not afford to do it entirely on their own, and after many legal delays the case was finally heard in July 1991.

It was the first time that damages had been sought in a murder in which there had been no conviction for murder. A similar case occurred in Los Angeles in February 1997, when O. J. Simpson lost an action for damages brought against him by the families of his murdered wife and her friend Ronald Goldman, although he had already been acquitted of their murder sixteen months before. The reason there can be such a reversal of verdicts is that in a civil case the standard of certainty required from the jury, or a judge, is lower. In a criminal trial the jury must be convinced 'beyond a reasonable doubt' that the person is guilty. In a civil case the decision is made on the balance of probability. In the O. J. Simpson damages case the jury were asked the question; 'Do you, by a preponderance of the evidence, find that O. J. Simpson wilfully and wrongfully caused the death of ...' and they replied: 'Yes.'

In the Michael Brookes case Mr Justice Rougier took two months to pass judgement, but eventually said: 'I had to ask myself whether the evidence convinced me that the real killer was [Michael] Brookes.' And the answer is: 'Yes, it has.' He ruled that the liability for damages was 20 per cent to Roy and 80 per cent to Michael.

But the victory for the Siddons family, arising from the trial and its outcome, raised an important legal question. If the Crown Prosecution Service now brought a charge of murder against Michael Brookes, in the light of all the publicity, could he receive a fair trial? This was answered when the Derbyshire police asked the Peterborough police to arrest him. In July 1992 he was brought before magistrates at Derby and charged with the murder of Lynn Siddons. His trial took nearly another four years to take place, after legal arguments which went eventually up to the House of Lords, but in June 1996 it began at the Old Bailey in London, eighteen years after the murder. On August 1st he was found guilty and sentenced to life imprisonment.

References
The Murder Yearbook, by Brian Lane, Headline, 1992
The Times
Derby Evening Telegraph

3

THE MURDEROUS MALE – MALE VICTIMS

Heterosexual Jealousy

The Bernard Walden Case

Jealousy is no respecter of persons and many men have become obsessed with a woman over the years, but thankfully few have resorted to murder. In April 1959, Bernard Walden was a 33-year-old lecturer in physics at Rotherham College of Technology. A brilliant student, he had suffered two misfortunes while at Oxford. His mother died and he contracted polio. The disease so interrupted his studies that he obtained only a third class degree and it left him with a withered left leg, a pronounced limp and a decided chip on the shoulder.

Nevertheless, to many young women Bernard Walden might have seemed a desirable boyfriend. He was good looking and his prospects must have been well above average. Yet 21-year-old Joyce Moran was unimpressed. Whether it was his physical deformity which put her off or whether she had some other objection to him we will never know, but whatever it was she rejected his advances.

Walden had first met her when he lodged near her home in Rotherham and he became a frequent visitor. He took her and her family for outings in his blue Ford Prefect and gave her lifts to work, since Joyce Moran was a typist in the college office. At some stage he asked her to marry him, but apparently she laughed off his proposal. A further shock awaited him when he went to Joyce's twenty-first birthday celebration and discovered that she had a boyfriend, 21-year-old Neil Saxton, who was a student at the college.

Matters came to a head on the evening of Tuesday April 7th. Bernard Walden was teaching a class when one of his students asked if he could let them have a copy of a previous year's exam paper to help them with their revision for this year's exams in a few weeks. He left the class to go to his locker and pick up a paper. But on the way he passed the office and saw young Neil Saxton leaning in through the window to talk to Joyce Moran who was sitting at her desk.

The sight incensed him. All the pent-up jealousy and feelings of rejection which he had experienced over the past few weeks welled up inside him and erupted in violence. Walden was a gun buff and kept weapons at his lodgings, in the boot of his car and even in his locker at the college. He went to the locker, took out a Luger pistol, and shot Neil Saxton in the back. Joyce began screaming. Walden went into the office, fired once and missed, but then shot her in the chest and fired another four bullets into her as she lay on the ground. Then he rapidly left the college.

When the police and ambulances arrived Joyce Moran was found to be dead and Neil Saxton died later in hospital. Bernard Walden was nowhere to be found. In fact he was not picked up for several weeks. He abandoned his car in Leeds and journeyed to Leicester and then on to London. He had quite a lot of money with him to begin with but this gradually dwindled and when he was finally discovered he was down to his last few coppers. He was seen by a policeman sleeping in a park shelter in Reading with a shotgun beside him, but he didn't use it and readily admitted who he was.

He was tried for the murder of Neil Saxton and Joyce Moran at Sheffield Assizes in June 1960. It was stated in court that Walden had a violent temper and, ten years before, had been charged with assaulting a boy with a poker. Attempts by the defence to have the charge reduced to manslaughter because of an abnormality of mind on the part of the accused were rejected by the jury who convicted him of murder and Walden was subsequently hanged in Armley Jail, Leeds.

References

Rotherham Star

Yorkshire Murder Casebook by Steve Fielding, Countryside Books, 1997

Homosexual Jealousy

The Joe Orton Case

Joe Orton is today famous for being a 1960s icon. The writer of the very successful plays *Loot, Entertaining Mr Sloan* and *What the Butler Saw* was at the time a famous, not to say anarchic figure, but today he would hardly raise an eyebrow. But if his life remains firmly rooted in the 1960s, his death could very much be a 1990s phenomenon.

In May 1951 two students enrolled at the Royal Academy of Dramatic Art. One was John Orton, 18, and the other Kenneth Halliwell who was twenty-five. They came from very different backgrounds. Joe came from a working-class family in Leicester and, although not a brilliant student at school, from an early age had been fascinated by the theatre and had won a scholarship to RADA. Kenneth's family were middle class and lived in the Wirral. He was an only child and when his doting mother died as a result of a wasp sting when he was eleven years old, he was devastated. His father committed suicide when Kenneth was twenty-one and he found himself with his father's savings and as the owner of a house. He failed to obtain a scholarship to RADA but was able to become a fee-paying student.

Kenneth and Joe soon met and were attracted to each other. Both were homosexual and were soon sharing Halliwell's rented flat and having an intense affair. Kenneth was very possessive and appointed himself as Joe's mentor, introducing him to expensive food, wine and books.

At the end of their courses Halliwell failed to get a diploma, but Joe did and they separated. Joe joined a repertory company in Ipswich and Kenneth one in Wales. But neither of them succeeded as an actor and they decided to get together again, to give up their careers and begin writing. They lived on the dole and Halliwell's inheritance, collaborating on novels and poems. At this stage in their relationship Kenneth was the leading figure, supplying the ideas and much of the text while Joe did the typing and made suggestions now and again.

Owing to Halliwell's rapidly dwindling inheritance they began working at Cadbury's West Hampstead depot for six months each year, Kenneth as a clerk and Joe as a packer, and then spent the rest of the year writing. None of the novels they wrote was ever published but they made enough money working in the depot to buy a small flat.

In 1959 they moved into a second-floor bed-sitting room at 25 Noel Road, Islington. The room was 16 feet by 12 and contained two divan beds, two easy chairs, two kitchen chairs and a desk which they shared. They kept very much to themselves, going out for walks in the nearby park or along the surrounding streets.

The 1960s was a time of youth protest and the beginnings of the gay rights movement. Up until 1967 homosexual acts had been illegal and participants could be imprisoned. At the beginning Orton and Halliwell's protest consisted of illicitly removing books from Islington library, taking out pictures or cutting out portions and replacing them with other illustrations culled from physical culture magazines. They would then surreptiously return the books to the shelves and hang around to watch the effect on elderly borrowers as they examined the books. They were eventually caught and for this rather childish activity received six months in prison each and were forced to pay Islington Borough Council substantial compensation.

Prison affected them differently. Halliwell was deeply humiliated and when he came out he tried to commit suicide. Orton, always mentally the tougher of the two, came out with a much more concentrated view of what he wanted to do. They began to write separately and in 1963 Joe adapted a story from one of their collaborations into a radio play and managed to sell it to the BBC. This was followed by the stage plays *Entertaining Mr Sloan* the following year and *Loot* in 1966. Both were black comedies in which violent and often surreal happenings take place in genteel surroundings. After *Loot* opened in the West End it became a great success, receiving the *Evening Standard* award and the *Plays and Players* award for the best play of 1966.

Joe Orton was feted by society, appearing on television on *Call My Bluff* and the *Eamonn Andrews Show*, being interviewed by newspapers and magazines and having his portrait drawn by a well-known artist. But the effect on Kenneth Halliwell was disastrous. From being the leader and adviser of the young Orton he had now been overtaken by his pupil. In addition the playwright never acknowledged Halliwell's help in public or even mentioned him, indeed giving out that his marriage had just broken up and he was now a single man.

Kenneth began to have fits of depression and tantrums and Joe recorded in his diary, which was always kept on the desk where Halliwell could see and read it, that he was becoming fed up with him. He also faithfully recorded his string of casual homosexual lovers which he usually picked in public toilets in the Holloway Road and King's Cross area.

In March 1967 Orton sold the film rights to *Loot* for £100,000 and in May Orton and Halliwell flew to Tangier, in those days a Mecca for homosexuals because of the availability of the local boys. They returned in July and on August 1st Orton wrote the last available entry in his diary. Subsequent pages were torn out and have never been found.

On August 9th a chauffeur-driven car drew up outside 25 Noel Road, Islington and the driver went up the stairs and knocked on the door of flat number 4. He had come to drive Joe to a lunchtime meeting with producer Oscar Lewenstein and film director Richard Lester. Orton had just sold Lewenstein the film rights to *Up Against It* for £10,000. But no-one answered the chauffeur's knock. He looked through the letter box. He could see the lights were on and what looked like the head of somebody on the floor. When the police broke in they found Halliwell lying on the floor. He had died from an overdose of barbiturates. On his bed was the body of Joe Orton in his pyjamas. His head had been smashed with severe blows from a hammer. He was thirty-four and Halliwell forty-one.

References
Prick Up Your Ears, by John Lahr
Murder Casebook, Vol 10, 147, Marshall Cavendish, 1993
The Times

Racial Prejudice

Byron de la Beckwith case

This story shows how time alters conceptions of justice and how public opinion changes over the years, encompassing different viewpoints, accepting some things and rejecting others. This type of situation, so far as I am aware, is not often dealt with in crime fiction, but I would have thought it to be a very fruitful one for ideas nevertheless.

Thirty-seven-year old Medgar W. Evers was a black man and a field secretary of the National Association for the Advancement of Coloured People. In the early hours of June 12th 1963 he arrived at his home on the northern outskirts of Jackson, Mississippi, after attending a mass meeting in a church in the city, convened to try and get the authorities to hire some black policemen. As he stepped out of his car and approached his front door he was struck in the back by a sniper's bullet and died twelve hours later in hospital.

His murder caused outrage all over America and President Kennedy said he was 'appalled by the barbarity of the act'. The FBI were soon on the case and only ten days later arrested 42-year-old Byron de la Beckwith, a native of Greenwood, Mississippi, in connection with the murder. It was said that he was a white segregationist and an extreme racialist, a member of the Sons of the American Revolution and the White Citizen's Coucil and one who had lectured to the Klu Klux Klan.

His first trial opened in Jackson, on January 31st 1964. Evidence was given by federal agents that the telescopic sight on the murder rifle, which was found near the scene of the crime, had been recently sold to Beckwith and indeed his fingerprint was still on it. Two white taxi drivers said that Beckwith was in Jackson four days before the murder asking where Evers lived and two other witnesses testified that they saw the accused's car parked a few hundred feet from the Evers home on the night of the murder.

Beckwith remained cheerful throughout the trial, perhaps believing that at the time a jury in Jackson would never find a white man guilty of killing a black. He went into the witness box to claim that his rifle had been stolen the day before the murder and his counsel was able to produce two policemen to testify that Beckwith was in Greenwood, a hundred miles from Jackson, when Evers was shot.

After nearly two days' deliberation the jury were unable to reach a verdict and Beckwith's second trial began a month later in the same place with the same judge and attorneys. The evidence was the same except that the local Klu Klux Klan sent its toughest members to hang around both inside and outside the court room and one of the taxi drivers, who had allegedly been beaten up, now said that he thought the man who asked directions to Evers's house might have been someone who merely looked like Beckwith. But the jury were again deadlocked and the state authorities decided against a third trial.

But in the 1990s the climate of opinion had changed in Jackson. There were now fears that the juries in the earlier Beckwith trials might have been tampered with and a former member of the Klu Klux Klan, turned FBI informer, claimed that Beckwith had boasted at Klan meetings that he had indeed shot Evers.

In January 1994, Byron de la Beckwith stood in the same court room as he had thirty-one years before, but the jury this time were drawn from a much wider area in Jackson, and on February 5th, after deliberating for six hours, they brought in a verdict of guilty and he was sentenced to life imprisonment.

References
Portrait of a Racist by Reed Massengill, St Martin's Press, N.Y.,1994
The 1995 Murder Yearbook by Brian Lane, Headline, 1994
Jackson Clarion-Ledger and News

Money

The Ernest Dyer Case
This is the story of two former officers from the First World War, a murder, a dream and an incredible ending. The officers were Lieu-

tenant Eric Tombe and Lieutenant Ernest Dyer. They met after the war when both worked at the Air Ministry. Eric Tombe was twenty-eight and fairly well off. His father was a parson and his parents lived in Sydenham, between Aylesbury and Oxford. Ernest Dyer was not so affluent, but he had plenty of business schemes and he persuaded Tombe to put his money into several, all of which failed.

In July 1920 Eric put up the money to buy The Welcomes stud farm near Kenley in Surrey. Subsequently Dyer lived on the farm with his wife and two children, although he was hardly ever there, and Tombe lived in Dorking. The venture lost money from the start and in April 1921 a mysterious fire destroyed most of the buildings. The insurance company were suspicious and declined to pay out and the partnership ended, Eric going to live in London.

Then Tombe disappeared. When his girlfriend returned from a trip she found Dyer, instead of Tombe, waiting to meet her at Euston Station. He handed her a telegram purporting to come from Eric in which he said he had gone abroad. She did not believe this and accused Dyer of writing it himself. He admitted it, but said he had done it at Tombe's request as he had gone off with another girl-friend.

It was perfectly true that Eric did have another girlfriend, but she had lost track of him too. She went to his flat and found Dyer there packing up Eric's things. He explained again that Tombe had gone abroad and this girlfriend believed him.

At about this time Eric's parents were becoming worried about him. They had not seen him for several months and his mother began having dreams in which he appeared to her. Eventually she had one in which she saw him again and thought that he was dead and at the bottom of a well.

The Reverend Tombe, who had already been in touch with Scotland Yard and had received only a visit from his local constabulary, went to London himself to try and get some information about his son. After fruitlessly advertising in the newspapers he eventually talked to a barber in the Haymarket, which both Tombe and Dyer had used regularly. He found out about Eric's partnership with Dyer, which he hadn't known of until then, and about the stud farm. With all this new information, including his wife's dream, he went to Scotland Yard again.

This time Superintendent Carling took charge of the case. He found that by forging Tombe's signature Dyer had emptied his partner's account at Lloyds Bank. He turned his attention to The Welcomes stud farm. In September 1923 the place stood abandoned and derelict and overgrown with weeds. The police found five wells and all had been filled with rubble and rubbish. They laboriously removed the debris from three and at the bottom of the third, buried in mud and rubbish was the body of Eric Tombe. Painstaking work by the pathologist determined that death had been caused by a shotgun wound to the back of the head.

The Metropolitan Police began a search for Ernest Dyer. Then they found that the previous November, almost a year before the body of Eric Tombe was discovered, the Scarborough police had gone to interview a man called James Fitzsimmons who was living in a hotel in the resort. There had been reports that he had been trying to get local businessmen interested in get-rich-quick schemes and passing dud cheques. As he was going up to his room, with two policemen following, he had suddenly reached inside his coat for a pistol. The police grappled with him. A shot rang out. And Fitzsimmons died on the hotel carpet. In his room they found blank cheques on which the name Eric Tombe had been pencilled and two service medals with the name Lieutenant E. Dyer stamped on the back. But whether Dyer shot himself deliberately or by accident remains a mystery.

References

Blind Justice? by Douglas Wynn, Robert Hale, 1990
Reminiscences Of An Ex-Detective by Francis Carlin, George H. Doran Co., New York
Scarborough Evening News and Daily Mercury
Daily News (London)
Daily Chronicle (London)

Revenge

The Fred Heyworth Case

Fred Heyworth, 59, was described by his son Rob Neil as 'an evil, domineering and uncaring person'. Heyworth had been adopted as a child by a wealthy family in Manchester and thus had many advantages that other children lack. He went on to start a successful printing business in Southampton and also organised a marching band. During the time he was in charge he had affairs with many of the young ladies in the band.

In 1979 he married one of them, Janette, after a divorce from his wife Rosemary. Janette was twenty-two years younger than he, but at first the marriage seemed satisfactory. They had two children and on the surface everything looked fine, although underneath their relationship was marred by a series of vicious assaults by Heyworth. After a final beating, on New Year's Day 1995, Janette finally left him and moved into her sister's home in Sholing, Southampton.

This came as something of a shock to Fred Heyworth. He was the one who left his women, not the other way round, and the loss of his wife was a considerable blow to his pride. He asked her to return, but she refused. She had had enough of the domination and the beatings. But Heyworth totally failed to understand her reasons for leaving. His ego would not let him believe that Janette was fed up with him. So he began to blame his sister-in-law Beverley Good. After Janette left, all he ever talked about whenever he saw his son Rob Neil was how she was being controlled by her sister. He became obsessed with the idea that it was all Beverley's fault.

The truth was that Beverely was a strong character. She stood up to Heyworth and gave her sister the support she needed, after years of violent domination, to put her life together again. But to Heyworth's twisted personality it was all Beverley's doing. She was the one who was poisoning his wife's mind against him. And Beverely's sisterly support was to cost her dear.

At a ladies' night at Heyworth's Masonic lodge, where his wife worked behind the bar, he made one last attempt to persuade her to come back. But again she said no. Then in the early hours of the morning he cycled to Sholing with a can of petrol in his hand. Silently he poured the petrol through the letter box of Beverley Good's house and set fire to it.

In the terrible conflagration which followed, Terry Good, 12, Nicola and Alison Good, who were eight and ten respectively, all died. Mr Justice Steel, sentencing Heyworth to life imprisonment after his trial on Friday May 16th 1997, said: 'What evil brainstorm prompted you to act as you did we shall never know.' But there are very good reasons to believe that it was a calculated act of revenge.

References
The Times
Daily Express
Southern Daily Echo

Sexual Gratification

The Peter Moore Case
Keith Randles, 49, was in charge of security at a roadworks site on the A5 at Mona, Anglesey and slept there in a caravan. When he was dragged from his bed by the tall, powerful Peter Moore and attacked with a knife he screamed: 'Why?'

'For fun,' snarled Moore.

Peter Moore was the only child of Edith and Ernest Moore of St Helens, near Liverpool. His mother was well into her forties when she had Peter and she adored him. The family moved to North Wales and Moore went to school in Towyn and Abergele, where he was teased about his height. The Moores had an ironmongery business in Kimmel Bay, near Rhyl, and Peter took it over when his parents retired. After his father died in 1979 he gave up the business and had a range of jobs, including running a hall where a baby clinic, dancing and carpet sales were held. He sold video tapes and gardening equipment and made deliveries of gas cylinders to caravan sites.

Then in 1991 he reopened an old cinema in Bagillt, Flintshire, doing all the repairs and refurbishment himself. He did the same with the Empire at Hollyhead and the Wedgewood at Denbigh. He called his chain Focus Cinemas and he seemed to be an extremely successful businessman. Friends and neighbours spoke of him as the perfect gentleman. Kind and considerate to old people, he would do anything to help anybody and was especially polite towards women.

But few if anyone knew about the secret life he led. A homosexual, he had an obsession with Nazi philosophy and gear and often wore black, especially when he went out at night looking for men. For over twenty years he terrorised his male victims – he was said to have attacked over fifty men – humiliating, beating and torturing them with various weapons. He and they were very lucky he did not actually kill anybody. But after his mother died in 1994, when he was fifty-four, this restraint seems to have been removed. He bought a flick knife from a shop in Rhyl and began an even worse reign of terror than the first.

His first victim was Henry Roberts, 56, a retired railway worker who lived by himself in a cottage near Caergeiliog, Anglesey. It was on Moore's route home from his cinema in Holyhead, which he would visit once or twice a week, usually late at night. Mr Roberts was found in September 1995 face-down outside his cottage with his trousers pulled down and stab wounds to both buttocks. He had also been stabbed fourteen times to his front and thirteen to his back. The second was Edward Carthy, 28, who met Moore in a gay bar in October of the same year. He too was stabbed to death and buried in the Clocaenog Forest, near Ruthin. Keith Randles, 49, died on November 30th 1995. He had fought for his life against the powerful Moore, but had eventually succumbed to repeated stab wounds. From him the killer stole a watch, a video recorder and a mobile telephone, all of which were later found in Moore's possession. The last victim was Tony Davies, who was a 40 year old crematorium worker. He had been married since 1983 and had two children. He was stabbed to death at Pensarn Beach, near Abergele, in December 1995.

It was said at Moore's trial that all the men he killed were complete strangers, who, according to his own confession, had done nothing to annoy or aggravate him. And in fact he was planning to take the life of a fifth man, his own bank manager, when arrested by the police. The detailed confessions taped in Llandudno police station included accounts of all the killings and referred to attacks made on other men dating back to the 1970s. They concluded with the words: 'I don't feel any remorse whatsoever for what I've done.' And Moore added that the killing 'relieved the pressure on him'.

During his trial, however, he claimed that the murders were done by a homosexual lover of his, whom he nicknamed 'Jason' after the killer in the *Friday the 13th* horror films. But the jury at Mold Crown Court in November 1996 did not believe him and required only just over two hours to deliver unanimous guilty verdicts on all four murder charges. Judge Maurice Kay said that Moore was as dangerous a man as it was possible to find and that he would be recommending to the Home Secretary that he should never be released.

References
The Times
Daily Express

In the Furtherance of Crime or to Escape

The Arthur Jackson case

The man who was being chased stopped and turned. His gun came up and he began walking towards the man who had been chasing him. It was a June day in 1967 and the confrontation took place in Knightsbridge. The gunman, Arthur Jackson, 31, had just attempted to rob the National Provincial Bank in Sloane Street, Chelsea, and been pursued down the road by Anthony Fletcher, 33, a self-employed contractor and former Grenadier Guardsman who lived in Wimbledon. Now, when it looked as if Jackson was cornered, he turned on his follower. Mr Fletcher backed away from the gun and a trace of fear appeared in his eyes. There was a sudden report and Anthony Fletcher clutched his chest. He collapsed on the pavement, blood running out from between his fingers.

Jackson, who had previously robbed a shop to obtain enough money to buy the gun, made his escape in the crowds of summer shoppers. Mr Fletcher subsequently died of his wound and was hailed as the first of Britain's 'have-a-go-heroes', the following year being posthumously awarded the George Medal for his very brave act. But he wasn't the first.

On a December day in 1944 three men jumped from a car in Birchin Lane in the City of London, smashed the window of a jeweller's shop and snatched trays of rings and a necklace. They roared off down the road with their booty. But incredibly a pedestrian stepped out into the road in front of them. He was 56-year-old Captain Ralph Binney, recently retired from the Royal Navy. He held out his arms and yelled: 'Stop.' But the car didn't and the gallant captain was dragged underneath it for more than a mile. He died soon after. His death was commemorated by a specially struck gold medal for bravery, called the Binney Medal. The award has been made every year since 1945 for the 'bravest action in support of law and order' by a person not connected with the police in the City of London and the Metropolitan Police areas.

Incidentally, one of the men subsequently convicted of the crime was Thomas Jenkins. In April 1947 Alec de Antiquis was shot dead on his motorcycle trying to stop three criminals who had just robbed a jeweller's shop in Charlotte Street. And one of the criminals convicted of that crime was Harry Jenkins, the younger brother of Thomas.

Arthur Jackson, a drifter who originally came from Aberdeen, was not captured in 1967 and made his way to America. He became obsessed with the Hollywood actress Theresa Saldana, who had starred in the film *Raging Bull*. And in 1982 he was convicted of trying to kill her and was sentenced to twelve years in prison.

Interviewed in prison by a British journalist in 1990 he boasted of the earlier killing of Mr Fletcher. When the murdered man's widow Valerie learnt that Jackson was in jail in California she began a campaign to have him extradited. This culminated in his appearing at the Old Bailey in January 1997, some thirty years after the murder. The court was told that Arthur Jackson, now classed as a paranoid schizophrenic, felt no remorse for killing Mr Fletcher, only 'pity, because of the look in the man's eyes of his impending doom'. He denied murder but admitted manslaughter on the grounds of diminished responsibility. This meant that he could be sent to a secure hospital. Mr Justice Potts said, 'As a result of your illness you are an exceptionally dangerous man and it is necessary that the hospital order be without limit of time for the protection of the public from serious harm.'

References

The Times

Real-Life Crimes, vol.8, Part 107, Eaglemoss Publications Ltd., 1995

Murder Casebook, vol.9, Part 125, Marshall Cavendish, 1992

For No Known Reason

The Matthew Hooper Case

This sad case was one of a disturbing trend at the time; that of allowing severely mentally disturbed patients out of hospital to be cared for in the community. A number of these cases ended in tragedy and this one was no exception. But from the point of view of the crime writer it does illustrate the reality of life very well. Crime writers often shy away from the motiveless crime, because the motive can play such an important part in the plot. But in real life there may be no discernible reason for a murder and the interest to the writer might be in the detailed mechanics of the investigation or the mental history of the murderer, both of which are outside the scope of this book.

Matthew Hooper was admitted to the Maudsley Hospital in southeast London, which has a record of important research in the statistical connection between epilepsy and murder, in April 1995. He had stabbed his brother and attacked his elderly mother. Hooper had a record of violence dating back to 1981. Diagnosed as a paranoid schizophrenic he was put on a regime of drugs and seemed to be responding well to treatment. He was discharged in July of the same year and was found a flat in East Dulwich by social services. But in November he was arrested for having a lock knife in his car, an old Ford Fiesta.

The authorities seemed to have ignored the warning signs because presumably Hooper had stopped taking his medication. Early on Christmas morning Hooper was involved in an altercation outside a public house in Peckham. His victim, 55-year-old Jack Trinder, a second cousin of the late comic Tommy Trinder, was stabbed 21 times in the chest and died on the way to hospital. Hooper made his escape in his car, which he afterwards set fire to on some waste ground to get rid of bloodstains. He also discarded his bloodstained clothing and abandoned his flat, moving in a with a friend. The final attempt to escape detection came when he grew a beard.

But witnesses who had seen the attack were able to describe Hooper and the car. And when the police found the wreck they were able to identify the owner from the licence records and the hunt was soon on for the killer. Hooper was eventually tracked down and arrested. He soon admitted the murder, and at his trial at the Old Bailey in November 1996 he pleaded manslaughter on the grounds of diminished responsibility. After his conviction Mr Justice Hawkins ordered that Hooper should be detained in Broadmoor without limit of time.

References

The Times

4

KILLER WOMEN

Killing Men for Love, Jealousy or Hate

The Tracie Andrews Case

It was at 11 o'clock at night on Sunday, December 1st, 1996 when the police reached a country lane near Alvechurch, just off the M42, not far from Bromsgrove. In the road by the side of a white Escort RS200 a woman was kneeling in the road, cradling the head of a man in her arms. Both were covered in blood, but the man was not breathing and appeared to be dead.

The woman said her name was Tracie Andrews and that she lived with her boyfriend Lee Harvey in Alvechurch. They had gone out for a drink, but on the way home they overtook a shabby, F registered, black Ford Sierra, which then proceeded to chase them. Both cars eventually stopped on Coppers Hill and Lee, who was driving, got out and had words with the driver of the Sierra. Subsequently the Sierra driver returned to his car, but then a passenger jumped out and began stabbing Mr Harvey, leaving him to die in the road. Tracie had tried to intervene, but had suffered a cut eyebrow and bruises.

She was taken to hospital and a search begun immediately for the black Sierra. The police appealed for witnesses and Tracie herself made an impassioned appeal on television for the driver, or anybody else in the black Sierra, to come forward.

Quite a number of witnesses did come forward, but nobody had seen a black Sierra. The police eventually set up eight roadblocks around the area and stopped and questioned 650 drivers, but they received no information about the missing car. Although a couple reported seeing Lee Harvey's white Escort that Sunday night driving home from the pub, they were sure that it was not being followed by another car. Another witness was a nine-year-old girl. She lived in a house which overlooked the murder site and was in bed asleep when she was woken by the sounds of an argument outside her house. It sounded like a man arguing with someone with a softer voice, like a woman. But she had heard no car drive away.

Another neighbour was a former detective constable, now a solicitor and who was one of the first on the scene, before the police arrived. She was suspicious from the start because although Tracie gave her the story of the road rage attack, she could not remember the colour, make or any part of the registration number of the car. But a few minutes later she heard Tracie tell the police it was an F registered black Sierra and heard her describe in detail the man who had attacked Lee.

The police decided to question Andrews again, but by this time she had taken an overdose of tranquillisers and was in hospital. She was arrested as soon as she was released, but the police had to delay questioning her because she was still too ill to be interviewed.

But the evidence was stacking up against her. Lee had been stabbed some thirty times with something like a small penknife. His jugular vein had been cut and unconsciousness would soon have overtaken him. The pattern of blood on Tracy Andrews's clothes suggested she had been close to him when the blood spurted from the vein, whereas she claimed she had been inside the car when he was attacked. Some parts of a small knife were actually found by the police underneath the body.

In addition the police discovered that the lovers' relationship had had a history of violence during its eighteen-month duration. The police had been called several times to their flat in Alvechurch to break up fights between them, and neighbours were always complaining of their loud and acrimonious arguments. A waitress in a nightclub remembered Tracie biting Lee on the neck during an argument and drawing blood. And a policeman saw her trying to attack him in the street late at night.

She was tried for murder at Birmingham Crown Court on June 30th 1997. The prosecution claimed that witnesses had seen them arguing at the pub on the night Lee died and the police theory was that she had given him a black woollen hat of the kind worn by blacks, as a joke, because he had a dark, Mediterranian complexion, and this had annoyed him. A black woolly hat was found near the scene of the murder, but at first Andrews denied knowing anything about it until cat hairs adhering to it were shown to come from her mother's pets.

But one of the most damming pieces of evidence was that she had made no attempt to raise the alarm for seventeen minutes at the murder scene, and only did so when a neighbour came out to get in his car. It was alleged that she used this time to concoct her story of the road rage attack.

Forensic evidence showed that three of Tracie's hairs had been clutched in Lee's hand and a clump of her hair, which was found nearby, clearly pointed to a fight between the two. The police never found the murder weapon, but forensic scientists examining Tracie's high heeled ankle-length fashion boots found the bloody imprint of a knife on the inside of the top part of one of them. It was suggested that she had concealed the knife in her boot and disposed of it in the hospital waste disposal when she went to the toilet there soon after the murder.

Her defence claimed that she wanted to marry Lee rather than kill him and persisted with the road rage attack theory, claiming that the police had not properly investigated that angle of the case. But the jury found her guilty of murder and she was sentenced to life imprisonment. An appeal against the conviction was made in October 1998, on the grounds that a miscarriage of justice had occurred because of the pre-trial publicity, but it was rejected.

References
The Times
Daily Express

Killing Men for Money

The Elfriede Blauensteiner Case

'Widow, early sixties, 1.65 metres, would like to share the quiet autumn of her life with a widower. I am a gardener, nurse, and a faithful companion.'

This advertisement appealed to 77-year-old retired postmaster Alois Pichler, who lived at Krems, thirty miles west of Vienna, Austria. He replied saying that he was lonely and well off and in no time at all he had met the widow, Elfriede Blauensteiner. Soon after, she moved in with him and two months later he was dead. His will, however, was in her favour. But the dead man's nephew was suspicious, since his uncle had never had a serious illness in his life. He went to the police and an autopsy revealed that the old man had died of heart failure brought on by the administration of Euglocon, a medicine for diabetics, and antidepressant tablets. It was alleged at the trial that after treating him with the cocktail of drugs in his bedtime hot chocolate over a succession of evenings she finally left Pichler in a room on a bitterly cold night with all the windows open. Then put him under a hot shower causing a fatal heart attack.

The police discovered that only four months before she met Pichler, her previous partner, a wealthy pensioner, had also died, leaving her very well off. But the motherly-looking 66-year-old Elfriede had a secret vice. She was a well-known figure at the casino at Baden, not far from Vienna, where she played most of the tables and was known to lose considerable sums of money at a time. She also dressed expensively, ate at the most exclusive restaurants and gave generous tips.

The police found that she had been the major benefactor in the deaths of at least five people: four men, including Pichler, and an elderly female neighbour who died in 1992 and left her a substantial amount of money. It was estimated that she had received in total some £1.2 million in property, securities and cash from her victims.

When she was interviewed by the police she confessed to poisoning them all. But when she went on trial in April 1997 she repudiated the confessions. She was charged with one specimen crime, the poisoning of Alois Pichler.

Her defence was that she actually hated men! Her father had died on the Russian front and her family, including six brothers, shared one room in Vienna. She claimed that she had an inbuilt fear of poverty and that after her first husband abandoned her and her daughter she developed a hatred of men. But the eight member jury had difficulty squaring this with her advertisements for male partners. Nevertheless it took them twelve hours of discussion to bring in a guilty verdict in which they stated that they believed her motives had been 'pure greed'. The 'Black Widow', as she became known during the trial, and not only because she wore black suits in court, was sentenced to life imprisonment.

References
The Times

Lest it be thought that the middle-aged to elderly female serial killer who murders for money is a very rare phenomenon it should be noted that in the nineteenth century, before there was a reliable test for arsenic, there were quite a number of women who used this method to get rid of husbands, elderly and wealthy relatives and even unwanted children. Even in the twentieth century there are a number of interesting cases.

Belle Gunness, who attracted men by a similar method to Elfriede Blauensteiner, had a farm in Indiana, USA. Until the farm burnt down in 1908 and she disappeared, she is known to have murdered eight men, probably with an axe, for their savings and there is a strong possibility there were six or seven more. Louise Peete had four husbands, and all four committed suicide. She shot two other men and a woman. Convicted of one murder in 1921 she served eighteen years and then emerged to commit another. She died in the gas chamber at San Quentin in 1947. South African Daisy De Melker poisoned two of her three husbands with strychnine and her grown-up son with arsenic. She was hanged in Johannesburg in October 1932.

References
Belle Gunness
The Mammoth Book of Killer Women by Richard Glyn Jones, Robinson, 1993
Lady Killers by Joyce Robins, Chancellor Press, 1993

Louise Peete
The Mammoth Book of Killer Women by Richard Glyn Jones,
Robinson, 1993
Daisy De Melker
Murder is my Business by Benjamin Bennett, Hodder & Stoughton,
1951

Killing Men for Sexual Gratification or Thrills

The Tracey Wigginton and Lisa Ptaschinski Case

This case illustrates an important aspect of murder: the influence of a group in the commission of a crime. Tracey Wigginton, Lisa Ptaschinski, Kim Jervis and Tracy Waugh were four lesbians in their twenties who lived in Brisbane, Australia, in 1989. In October of that year the four women sat in a nightclub of that city and planned a murder.

Tracey Wigginton was undoubtedly the leader. She had a large frame – she weighed 17 stones – and had a personality to match, although she had been physically and sexually abused as a child. Lisa Ptaschinski was a very disturbed young woman, having been admitted to Brisbane hospital 82 times in five years for conditions varying from heroin abuse to suicide attempts. But she was fascinated and dominated by Wigginton, as were the other two. Kim Jervis was heavily into occult practices and so obsessed by death that she had a gravestone stolen from a cemetery in the hallway of her flat. Tracey Waugh was a shy withdrawn girl whose lesbianism drew her to Kim Jervis and Tracey Wigginton. But they were all under the spell of magic and superstition and the three girls claimed at their trial that Tracey would eat only blood, either from pigs or cattle, and that the object of the murder they planned was to supply Wigginton with human blood.

On Friday night, October 20th, the four set out in Tracey Wigginton's car looking for a suitable victim. She had a knife and so had Jervis. They saw a drunk clinging to a lamp post and Wigginton and Jervis got out to ask him if he would like a lift home. His name was Edward Baldock and he was 47 years old. But instead of driving him home they went to Orleigh Park and after offering him sex Wigginton walked alone with Baldock down to the river bank near the South Brisbane Sailing Club. There they both undressed. Wigginton had previously told the others she would strangle the victim with her bare hands, but she came back to the car asking for help. Ptaschinski went back with her after receiving a knife from Jervis. Lisa went behind Baldock, who was sitting naked, apart from his socks, on the ground and Wigginton told her to stab him. But she could not. Wigginton then stabbed him several times in the throat and neck. She told Ptaschinski to return to the car and later rejoined the others saying, according to them, that she had fed on the blood.

They drove off thinking that they had committed the perfect murder. But they hadn't. Edward Baldock, perhaps suspecting that he might be robbed by the girls, had secretly placed his wallet behind one of the metal up-and-over doors of the boat house. And in addition he had found Tracey Wigginton's bank card when he was alone and slipped it into one of his shoes that he had taken off.

On the way home the four young women were stopped by the police in a routine check of cars. But when the body of Edward Baldock was found a few hours later, with fifteen stab wounds, and the bank card discovered in the shoe, it did not take the police long to match this with the registered owner of the car stopped the night before. Tracey Wigginton was soon in police custody. Lisa Ptaschinski gave herself up and soon after, Jervis and Waugh were arrested.

Wigginton confessed to the crime, but she underwent extensive psychiatric examination because the state wanted to determine whether she was legally insane when she committed the murder. Eventually the Queensland Mental Heath Tribunal decided that she was legally sane and in January 1991 she pleaded guilty to murder and was given a life sentence.

But the spectacular trial came the same month when Ptaschinski, Jervis and Waugh were tried together for murder. They pleaded not guilty and blamed everything on Tracey Wigginton who they claimed had manipulated them by fear. But after fifteen days of hearing evidence the jury found Ptaschinski guilty of murder, Jervis of manslaughter and they acquitted Waugh. Ptaschinski received a life sentence and Jervis eighteen years.

References

Courier-Mail, Brisbane

The Sun, Brisbane

Murder Casebook, vol. 6, Part 83, Marshall Cavendish, 1991

Killing Women for Love, Jealousy or Hate

The Heather Arnold Case

This case is of particular interest to crime writers because it shows how the investigator can interpret the crime scene to obtain information about the person who committed the crime or perhaps the state of mind they were in at the time.

On Wednesday afternoon, April 30th 1986, Paul Sutcliffe, a 45-year-old maths teacher, who lived in Westbury in Wiltshire, collected three of his children from school and drove them home. But a terrible surprise awaited them. In the house lay the bodies of Sutcliffe's wife and his eight-month-old daughter Heidi. They had been literally hacked to death with some heavy sharp instrument like an axe. Mrs Sutcliffe had received thirteen blows, mostly to the head and face and even little Heidi had a throat wound.

What possible motive could the killer have for destroying the child, who was far too young even to be a witness who could give the killer away? The fashion in which Mrs Sutcliffe's face had been attacked and the young child murdered pointed to someone who wanted not just to kill them but to utterly destroy them. Facial wounding often indicates that the attacker knows and is known to the victim. But who would harbour such hate for the pair?

The person the police suspect first, in crimes like this, is the husband, since in the majority of cases he is found to be the culprit.

But Paul Sutcliffe was soon eliminated since his time at school could be fully accounted for all day. Then there was the possibility that Mrs Sutcliffe had an enemy. Someone who hated her enough to want to kill her. But Sutcliffe could think of no-one. Or was this a crime directed at the husband, a revenge attack on something he loved, for some injury he had done the murderer? Did he have, for example, a lover who might have become insanely jealous of his wife? But he repudiated such a suggestion and no evidence could be found that he had had such an affair. He claimed that he had no enemies, but he did point out that he had recently told colleagues that he had decided to give up his job as head of maths at Kingsdown School in Warminster to join his wife Jeanne in converting her dressmaking hobby into a business. Most of his colleagues wished him the best of luck, but his deputy's attitude had been ambivalent. She was 50-year-old Heather Arnold and she was the only one of his close colleagues who had not sent a card or a letter of sympathy to the family after the murder.

She had lived on her own since her divorce and her only child, her daughter, had married and moved away to Staffordshire. In fact she lived not far from the Sutcliffes. Paul had always had a friendly relationship with Heather, helping her with the move after the divorce and occasionally doing odd jobs for her. But he said that there had been no romance. The police however were intrigued. What if there had been a desire for a love affair on her part and Paul's impending move meant the end of her hopes? Would that have been enough?

Detective Superintendent Tony Burden had only his hunch to go on; he had nothing against Heather Arnold, but he knew he would have to do something soon. He discovered that her dustbin was due for collection by the council in a few days time. And when the lorry rumbled up to her door, unbeknown to her, some of the dustbin men were police officers in disguise. At the bottom of one of her plastic bags was the handle of a small axe. It was blackened as if someone had tried to burn it and it had been sawn into three pieces.

The police decided to interview Heather Arnold, but by this time she had gone to stay with her daughter in the Midlands. And it was there that she showed her daughter the axe head she had used. Her son-in-law got in touch with the police in Wiltshire and on the way back in a police car, according to the police, she confessed the crime to a woman officer.

At her trial, which began at Bristol Crown Court on April 1st 1987, she retracted her confession and substituted an alibi saying that she was innocent of the crime. But forensic testing of the axe head showed that although it had been boiled to get rid of evidence, tiny traces of blood identical to Mrs Sutcliffe's could still be found on it. A single hair, said to be the same as those from the victim's head, was also discovered as well as a minute spot of hair lacquer of the kind used by Mrs Sutcliffe. And very small particles of the paint on the axe were found in the wounds of both mother and child.

The jury found her guilty by a unanimous verdict and she received a life sentence. Some years later during interviews with psychiatrists she told them that she had been depressed and had an antipathy to Mrs Sutcliffe whom she believed was trying to stop her becoming close to Paul. She was advised by psychiatrists to appeal against the verdict, claiming a defence of diminished responsibility. But this was rejected by the Court of Appeal when it was heard in February 1996, and she remains in prison.

References
The Times
Real-Life Crimes, vol. 8, Part 120, Eaglemoss Publications Ltd., 1993

The Susan Christie Case
It is difficult to say what the motives were in this killing; jealousy, certainly, hate possibly, and also revenge, or it might have been a straightforward removing of an obstacle to future happiness. But for the crime writer it does show that in real life motives are sometimes mixed and often difficult to discern precisely.

Susan Christie was a 21-year-old private in the Ulster Defence Regiment, stationed at Portadown in Northern Ireland. In 1989 she joined the sub-aqua club run by Duncan McAllister, a captain in the Royal Signals Regiment. It seems that she had a crush on him and he eventually learned of this through another officer. His own version of the subsequent events are that he approached her and dispassionately asked if she wanted an affair with him, pointing out the dangers involved and also telling her that he was a married man who wouldn't leave his wife. They then agreed to have an affair, which started slowly at first and then one day by the side of a lake they found that they were making love.

Susan's version is somewhat different. She agreed that Duncan approached her first and that it took her some time to make up her mind to go out with him, although she was very much attracted to him. She said that she was reluctant to make love since she was a virgin but that the captain pursued her relentlessly and eventually seduced her upstairs in his own home. She said that she became pregnant late in 1990, but that McAllister told her that she must have an abortion or he would leave her and claim that the child was not his. But in December 1990 she suffered a miscarriage.

In the spring of 1991 Susan Christie was accepted for officer training, which would entail a stay at the Royal Military College, Sandhurst. Duncan took this opportunity to tell her that he would not leave his wife and that their affair was over. Susan seemed to take this quite calmly, but a few days before she was due to leave she invited Penny, McAllister's wife – they seemed to have been on friendly terms in spite of the affair – to take their dogs for a walk in Drumkeeragh Forest park. But Susan arrived without her dogs ...

At about 1.30 p.m. Christie was seen staggering from the trees. There was blood all over her and she had some wounds to her legs. She said that Penny had gone on ahead following one of the dogs while she stopped to tie her shoelace. She heard screams and saw a man standing over Penny. When she came up he attacked her and she thought she was going to be raped, but the man ran off. Penny was found to be dead, her throat cut from ear to ear, apparently with a very sharp knife. The police made a helicopter search of the woods and set up road blocks, but there was no trace of the man.

It was four days later when Duncan McAllister confessed to the police that he had had an affair with Susan. The police questioned Susan again and at first she denied having an affair, but then admitted it. Eventually she made a kind of confession, acknowledging that there had been no man there, but saying she could not remember what had happened.

She was tried for murder at Downpatrick Crown Court in June 1992. She offered a plea of guilty to manslaughter on the grounds of diminished responsibility, but the prosecution would not accept this and the trial proceeded on a charge of murder. A pathologist stated that in his opinion Penny's head had been jerked back, exposing her throat which had been cut in one movement. Expert testimony suggested that a butcher's knife found 200 yards from the scene was the murder weapon and that it had been honed after purchase to give it a sharper edge.

In her testimony Susan still maintained she could not recall attacking Penny, but on cross-examination accepted that she had killed her. 'I would say I killed her for Duncan. I meant to get Duncan for myself. I was that in love with him I would have done anything.'

The judge summed up in her favour, saying: 'Can you conceive of a girl of her background going into a shop and sharpening a knife and carrying out this vicious act of killing if she had not taken leave of her senses?' Clearly the jury agreed, because she was found not guilty of murder, but guilty of manslaughter. The judge then sentenced her to five years' imprisonment. This meant that, allowing for the time she had spent on remand before the trial, plus remission, she could be free within a year.

The sentence caused an uproar and the Director of Public Prosecutions appealed against the sentence to the Northern Ireland Court of Appeal. In November 1992 Susan Christie's sentence was increased to nine years. In the same month Captain Duncan McAllister was asked to resign his commision, which he did. Susan Christie was freed in September 1995.

References

Deadly Jealousy by Martin Fido, Headline, 1993
The 1994 Murder Yearbook by Brian Lane, Headline, 1993
The Times
Portadown Times

5

MISCELLANEOUS MURDER

People who Kill Patients under their Care

The Nurse Genene Jones Case

The doctor in the hospital at the little town of Comfort, forty miles from San Antonio in southern Texas, was puzzled. It was September 23rd, 1982, and a five-month-old baby girl had just been brought in after she had stopped breathing while being given intravenous treatment for dehydration at Dr Kathleen Holland's clinic in the town. After resuscitation the baby began breathing, but seemed to be making movements very similar to those of a patient treated with succinylcholine. This drug is used to paralyse the heart muscles during cardiac surgery and would not be used on a child as young as this because it could arrest the heart. It was then recalled at the hospital that a number of very young children had been brought from Dr Holland's clinic, which had been opened for only four weeks, suffering from similar symptoms and many of them had died. Only six days before, fifteen-month-old Chelsea McClellan had died on the way to hospital after suffering a seizure at the clinic while under the care of 32-year-old Nurse Genene Jones.

Young Dr Holland was asked to come to the hospital and was questioned about the drug. She said that she had never used succinylcholine on young children. When she got back to the clinic she examined her supplies and found two apparently full vials of the drug, in solution, but the cap of one had puncture marks as if someone had pushed a hypodermic syringe into it to withdraw some of the contents. In addition her records showed that she should have had three vials.

She questioned her nurse Genene Jones about it, but she said she had no knowledge of what had happened to the drug. However, a short time later Jones took an overdose and was rushed to hospital. Dr Holland reported all this to the doctors at the hospital who put it in the

61

hands of the Texas Rangers, the investigatory arm of the state police, and the two vials were sent for analysis.

Nurse Jones was interviewed in hospital, but she denied any involvement in the deaths of the young children and the State District Attorney, who was now in charge of the case, realised that it would be very difficult to prove anything about the deaths: succinylcholine is broken down so rapidly in the body that there was very little chance of finding any after death. But the results of the analyses of the vials from Dr Holland's clinic showed that someone had removed over half of the contents of one and replaced it with water.

The DA consulted the pathologist in San Antonio who had performed the autopsy on Chelsea McClellan and when pressed she agreed that the symptoms could be that of the administration of succinylcholine, but they could result from other things as well. However, a colleague who had worked at the Medical Centre Hospital in the city the previous year, when there had been an outbreak of sudden infant deaths, recognised the names Dr Holland and Nurse Genene Jones.

An enquiry was launched by the DA and it was discovered that one of the measures taken by the hospital to halt the epidemic was to get rid of all licensed vocational nurses, one of whom was Nurse Genene Jones. It was after this that Dr Holland opened her clinic in Comfort and asked Jones to become her nurse.

Nurse Jones appeared before a Grand Jury in San Antonio in February, 1983, and self-confidently denied being involved in any way with the deaths at the Medical Centre Hospital; and the evidence against her was very slim. Then District Attorney Ron Sutton heard of a Swedish scientist, Dr Bo Holmstedt, who claimed to be able to detect succinylcholine using the sensitive technique gas liquid chromatography. Chelsea McClellan's body was exhumed and tissue samples sent to Dr Holmstedt for analysis. The results were positive.

By this time Nurse Jones had disappeared, but she was traced and arrested by the Texas Rangers and brought to trial in January 1984. After four weeks she was found guilty of murdering Chelsea McClellan and sentenced to life.

Some of her colleagues claimed that Genene Jones was over-bearing and overconfident of her understanding of children's medical problems, while others were impressed by her ability and her devotion to her patients. Whatever the truth of the matter, from the point of view of the crime fiction writer, the situation of a murderer who actually works in a hospital must be an intriguing one, since the perpetrator of the crimes is so difficult to detect.

Beverley Allitt, in a little under two months, working in the children's ward at Grantham Hospital in 1991, managed to murder four children. She was also found guilty of attempting to murder three more and of inflicting grievous bodily harm on a further five.

References

Nurse Genene Jones
The Death Shift by Peter Elkind, Corgi, 1990
San Antonio Light, Texas

Beverley Allitt
Murder on Ward Four by Nick Davies, Chatto & Windus, 1993

People who kill Children under their Care

The William Jennings Case

This is a particularly interesting case for crime writers for it shows two important aspects of a real life murder. The first is that to get a conviction the police, who may have a strong suspicion who the murderer is, may have to resort to subterfuge. And the second is the importance of applying the latest techniques of forensic science to a difficult problem.

It was on December 12th 1962 that 25-year-old William Jennings reported that his three-year-old son Stephen was missing. Jennings lived with his wife and three other children, Paul, 4, Susan who was two, and baby Barry who was only four months old, in a small terrace house in the village of Lower Gomersal between Batley and Cleckheaton in West Yorkshire. He said that he had been looking after the three eldest children while his wife took baby Barry to the local clinic. The three eldest had gone out to play and only Paul and Susan had returned.

But nobody believed him. Everyone in the village knew that the children were neglected. They were often seen in the streets inadequately clothed and asking for food. And Stephen always seemed to be the target of his father's anger. It was popularly believed that William thought he wasn't the father of the child, since he had been born while William was in prison for theft. And indeed Stephen had been admitted to hospital the year before with badly scalded feet when he had been left in the house alone with William.

Everybody was convinced that William was responsible for Stephen's disappearance. Nevertheless the search for the little boy was intense. All the men in the village and all the local police joined in as the weather that winter was bitter. But little Stephen could not be found. The region was an old industrial area with disused mine shafts, deep pools of oily water and ancient railway tunnels. But everything was searched. Police frogmen dived in freezing water and men, including William Jennings, tramped across the wasteland and the hillsides. But it was all to no avail and eventually the search was scaled down and subsequently discontinued. However it surfaced occasionally. When the Moors murderers Ian Brady and Myra Hindley were arrested Stephen's name was added to the list of missing children they might have killed.

William Jennings had been seen that day with a sack over his shoulder. But he maintained that his son had been abducted by gypsies and he stuck to his story even though he was interviewed intensively by the police who didn't believe him any more than the villagers did. But there was no evidence against him, and since he wouldn't budge on his position, finally he was released.

Then, in April 1988, twenty-five years after young Stephen had disappeared, a man walking his dog only three quarters of a mile from the old home of the Jennings family came across a small human skull at the bottom of a hedge by a dry stone wall. He looked further and found some small bones. He looked no more, but got in touch with the police, because he knew who it was, the disappearance still being common knowledge in the village. The police called in Dr John Hunter from Bradford University who was a pioneer in the new technique of forensic archaeology and his team carefully disinterred the bones. They found a small pair of leather sandals, which hadn't rotted away like all the other clothing and the sack, and these were of the same type young Stephen had been wearing when he disappeared. Examination of the bones by the Home Office pathologist at St James's Hospital in Leeds showed a greenstick fracture of one wrist which Stephen was known to have suffered and the teeth showed that the skeleton was of a 3 to $3^{1}/_{2}$ year old child.

By this time the old home in Gomersal had been replaced by new bungalows and William and his wife had separated after they had both served prison sentences for the neglect of their children. Jennings was found to be living near Wolverhampton. But the police decided on a policy of secrecy, hoping that they could confront the father with the discovery of his son without his having heard about it beforehand through the press, and that the shock might provoke a confession. Nevertheless the streetwise Jennings, who had been in and out of jail all his life, initially did not break down, merely sticking to his original story. But on the way back to Batley in the police car he did confess, saying that really it was an accident. He had pushed the boy and he had fallen downstairs. He had tried the kiss of life, but the boy stopped breathing, and in a panic he dumped the body in a sack by a wall and covered it with stones.

This was his story at his trial in May 1989 at Leeds Crown Court. But expert examination of the bones contradicted this account, suggesting that the little boy had suffered a very severe beating, which would undoubtedly have killed him straightaway. William Jennings was found guilty of murder and sentenced to life imprisonment. A subsequent appeal was dismissed.

References

The Times
Real-Life Crimes, vol.2, Part 29, Eaglemoss Publications Ltd., 1993
Spenborough Guardian

Murder by Paedophiles (of Children not under their Care)

Operation Orchid

This case – it is really a series of cases, called by the police Operation Orchid – illustrates an important feature of many investigations, where a word here and there leads from person to person until finally the truth emerges. Unfortunately the almost total lack of forensic evidence linking the suspects to the crimes in this case meant that the usable evidence was almost entirely from more or less unsatisfactory witnesses, so that the end result was not what most people, including the police, hoped for.

The body of fourteen-year-old Jason Swift was found in a field near Stapleford Tawney, Essex, in November, 1985. He was naked and had been the victim of a violent sexual assault before being suffocated. The boy had had a troubled childhood, spending much of his life in care and at the time of his disappearance, during the previous July, he had been living with his sister. He was known to move in homosexual circles, it being thought that he might be a rent boy, and the police suspected that Jason's killer also came from this world.

A few days later the body of another young boy was discovered, this time near Waltham Abbey in Essex. He was Barry Lewis, of mixed race, and was only six. He had disappeared from his mother's home at Walworth, south London. Analysis of the tissues showed traces of diazepam, temazepam and desmethyldiazepam, all drugs used by homosexuals as relaxants during intercourse. And when toxicological examination of Jason Swift's body showed the same drugs the police realised the cases were probably linked. But apart from a motorist who remembered giving a lift to a man and a young boy, whom he recognised as Barry and who appeared to be ill, near Waltham Abbey, the police had little evidence to go on and subsequently all leads petered out.

In 1987 a paedophile ring was broken up in London when the members all received prison sentences for buggery and indecent assault. Two members, Sidney Cooke and Lennie Smith, both came from the same Hackney estate where Jason Swift had lived, but they angrily denied knowing him. The same year a family living in Hackney complained that a man who had been babysitting for them had sexually assaulted their four-year-old son. The man admitted the crime and also began to talk about other men who had abused children. He knew Jason Swift and said a man closely associated with Jason was called Robert Oliver.

Oliver was picked up at the flat of his friend Leslie Bailey, who was nicknamed 'Catweazle' because of his thin features and staring eyes. Oliver said he had been introduced to Jason by Sidney Cooke and Lennie Smith. And after questioning by the police Oliver and Bailey both confessed to being involved, with other men, in the death of Jason Swift. At the trial in March 1989 Cooke was sentenced to nineteen years, Oliver and Bailey to fifteen and a man called Stephen Barrell to thirteen years. Lennie Smith was acquitted.

Drugs which had been found in Barry Lewis's body were also found in Oliver's flat. The police were convinced that this gang had been involved in Barry's murder. Two months after the trial a prisoner in Wandsworth Prison who was sharing a cell with Bailey reported that Bailey had confessed to a number of child murders (he said twenty to twenty-five, but detectives considered that eight to ten might be a more realistic figure). One of these victims was Barry Lewis.

Detectives visited Bailey in jail and eventually he admitted that Barry had been killed at a flat on the Kingsmead Estate in south London. The young boy was placed in the back of a car and Bailey told to dump the body. As he was driving along he looked in his rear-view mirror and saw the boy get up – he wasn't dead, merely drugged. Soon after that he ran out of petrol and had to take the child by the hand and hitchhike to a garage for petrol. Later he suffocated the little boy with a blanket and buried the body in a field. In June 1991 he was convicted of murder and jailed for life.

His conviction led Cooke, Oliver and Barrell to appeal against the length of their sentences. The appeal court agreed that the judge who sentenced them would not have given them such long sentences had he known of the extent of Bailey's involvement. Cooke's was reduced to sixteen years and Barrell's to ten. Oliver's appeal was dismissed.

During Bailey's many confessions to his fellow inmates he had commented on how easy it was to pick up children at fairgrounds and he revealed how he had become a fairground worker for that purpose. Cooke was also a fairground worker. Detectives then remembered the case of Mark Tildesley, a seven-year-old boy who had disappeared from a fairground at Wokingham, Berkshire, in 1984. During the investigation into his disappearance a fairground worker had told the police he had sold a Jaguar car to Sidney Cooke on hire purchase terms and when Cooke defaulted on the payments he repossessed the car. Among the many items left on the back seat he had seen a key ring fashioned into an Esso tiger. But the feet had broken off. Mark's parents confirmed that he had such a ring, but by this time it had been thrown out by the fairground worker.

Bailey told how he and Lennie Smith had received a telephone call from Cooke telling them to go to Wokingham. They had driven there to find that Cooke had a young boy. He was subsequently drugged in the usual way and eventually strangled, but Bailey didn't know what happened to the body afterwards. Mark's body has never been recovered and indeed no-one has been charged with his murder.

In 1993 Leslie Bailey was strangled to death in Whitemoor maximum security prison in Cambridgeshire.

References

The Times
The Daily Mirror (who mounted their own investigation and claimed that Lennie Smith, who had been jailed for ten years for sexually abusing a six-year-old boy, had been involved in the murder of Jason Swift)
Daily Star
The Sun

Mass Murder

The Michael Bryant Case

Mass murder and serial killing are discussed in the *Crime Writer's Handbook*. It need only be said here that mass murder usually means killing a number of people in a relatively short space of time, probably no more than a few hours, and serial killing involves the victims being dispatched one at a time over periods that may range from a few days to several years.

Michael Bryant, who was twenty-eight at the time, fitted many of the characteristics of a mass murderer. He was a young loner and a misfit in the close-knit community of Hobart, the capital of Tasmania. He had a disturbed family background and like most of this kind of murderer harboured a grudge against society, or certain parts of society. He was unusual in that many mass killers turn their anger against their family or work mates, fellow students, etc. Bryant attacked tourists, people he did not know. And mass murderers often do not avoid capture, sometimes shooting it out with the police until they are killed or commit suicide themselves – and in fact many mass killing episodes appear to be elaborate suicide missions in which the murderer determines 'to take as many people with him as he can'. But Bryant, after trying to avoid capture for some time, eventually gave himself up.

It is difficult to say when it all began. Clearly something of the kind must have been in his mind for many months, since he began building up a supply of ammunition and hiding his semiautomatic rifles in a piano in his home a long time before he began his killing orgy. And on the evening of Saturday, April 27th 1996, Bryant had dinner with his mother and girlfriend and neither of them noticed anything unusual.

The next day he set out for Port Arthur in his yellow Volvo with his surf boards strapped on a roof rack. He stopped for petrol on the way and two witnesses asked him if he was going surfing.

'No,' he said. 'I am going to the Island of the Dead to get rid of some wasps.'

Presumably he meant WASP ('White, Anglo-Saxon, Protestant,') a derogatory term that originated in the USA and Canada. Port Arthur, on the southern coast of Tasmania, used to house a penal colony and the grounds are now a tourist attraction. Across the bay lies the Island of the Dead, the cemetery where nineteen-century convicts were buried.

Bryant's first port of call was the small 'Seascape' guest house near the grounds, where he shot and killed the elderly couple who ran it, David and Sally Martin. Then he went to the Broad Arrow cafeteria, just outside the entrance to the former penal colony. There must have been forty or fifty people inside and Bryant opened fire with his semiautomatic rifle. It is estimated that his first burst killed a dozen diners, and witnesses said that Bryant began laughing as terrified patrons dived to the floor under tables to avoid the hail of bullets. He went from table to table carefully shooting at people lying on the floor. In a matter of minutes, when Bryant left the cafe, twenty were dead and a further eighteen badly injured.

The gunman then rushed outside to where a tourist bus was waiting and shot and killed the driver, two passengers and a bystander. On the other side of the toll booth stood a young mother and her two daughters. She was holding the three-year-old in her arms when Bryant opened fire at them. The six-year-old girl ran behind a tree, but Bryant in his deadly game of hide-and-seek followed and cut her down with a bullet to the back of the neck.

Back up the the road he went, firing indiscriminately at cars as they passed and people walking. He couldn't have chosen a better day to carry out his slaughter as the narrow country lanes were crowded with holiday traffic. At some stage he must have realised that the police would soon be on his trail, for he took a male hostage and as the first police car arrived at the 'Seascape' guest house, where the tragedy had begun, the occupants were met by gunfire from the house. The policemen jumped from their car and took shelter in a nearby ditch.

A television journalist reported that she had a telephone conversation with the gunman during the siege. When she rang the guest house

Bryant told her he was having a lot of fun, but that he wanted to have a shower and if she rang again he would shoot his hostage. The siege went on for seventeen hours, but in the early hours on Monday morning the guest house burst into flames and Bryant dashed out with his clothes on fire.

He was severely burned and subsequently required plastic surgery, but he had left behind three bodies in the guest house, which was completely gutted by the fire, the two Martins and the hostage.

Michael Bryant was accused of the murder of thirty-five people at a hearing in Tasmania's Supreme Court in Hobart, where he sat behind a bulletproof screen. He faced seventy-two separate charges and pleaded guilty to every one. The whole country heaved a sigh of relief since this saved the relatives of the victims the trauma of a trial. Bryant was sentenced to life without the possibility of parole. It was the worst shooting incident Australia had ever encountered and probably the worst even on a world scale, not counting military and ethnic massacres.

References

The Times

The Mercury, Hobart

The Australian

Mob or Gang Violence

The Learco Chindamo Case

St George's Roman Catholic School, a secondary comprehensive in Maida Vale, north-west London, was, in December 1995, a tough school in a tough area. It bordered the wealthy suburb of St John's Wood, but took many pupils from the council estates of Kilburn and Maida Vale. Street gangs were endemic in the area, some of them modelling themselves on the traditional Chinese organisations, the Triads, although they took as members a multinational mix of teenagers, some as young as thirteen. One gang was known as Woo Sang Wu (WSW) and was composed mostly of Filipino youths. They wore loose dark jackets to conceal knives and other weapons and bandannas round their heads or faces, and they usually fought gangs of blacks.

It was on Monday December 4th when Christopher Gan, a Filipino who was fourteen and a member of the WSW, considered he'd been jostled in the school corridor by a black thirteen-year-old. They started a fight, which was broken up by teachers. But it continued outside in the school yard, off and on, for several days. Both were threatened with expulsion if they carried on, but Gan was not going to let it rest there. He got in touch with Learco Chindamo, the leader of his gang.

Chindamo, whose natural father was an Italian gangster, currently serving a fifteen-year sentence in Italy for throwing sulphuric acid in a woman's face, had a Filipino mother, a stepfather and two brothers. He lived in Camden and went to Quinton Kynaston School in St John's Wood. He organised the proposed attack on the thirteen-year-old, carefully. The gang of twelve members were to be split into three groups so as not to arouse suspicions. They would collect in streets near the school and when the black boy came out on the following Friday afternoon he would be lured, on the pretext of going to the recreation ground, into their clutches.

But it all went wrong. The young boy was suspicious and as soon as he saw youths with scarves over their faces across the road he ran back to the school. He tried to ring a friend's older brother from the school, but couldn't get through. The deputy head could see that the boy was distressed and came over to him. He was soon joined by the head himself, Philip Lawrence. But the boy, obeying the strict code of the streets, would not say what the matter was. They accompanied him to the school gates. There Gan demanded that he fight. Philip Lawrence remonstrated, but the tension was high among the crowd outside the school.

The black boy was suddenly hit on the head by an iron bar one of the gang was carrying and he ran off. As Lawrence made to follow he was confronted by Chindamo who struck him in the face and kicked him. But Lawrence came forward again and to bystanders it looked as if he was then punched in the chest. This time the headmaster staggered back clutching his breast. Although he was wearing a heavy overcoat, blood was seeping through his fingers. He turned into the school gates, but soon collapsed. Children supported him in their arms, but although an ambulance was quickly called he died later in hospital.

Philip Lawrence was forty-eight and had been headmaster for three years. A committed Catholic, he had a good academic background and was an enthusiastic teacher and a strong leader. When he first came to the school, which wasn't a large one, having only 440 pupils and staff, its academic record was poor. But he got rid of the unruly element, expelling twenty-five pupils, and brought in young and enthusiastic teachers and by the time he died the school had become a favourite among local parents.

Even though the rule of not talking to the police was a strong one on the streets, the police took only four weeks to track down Learco Chindamo. After being arrested, hiding in a flat in Kentish Town, he was brought to trial for murder at the Old Bailey in September 1996. Witnesses described what had happened, even some members of his own gang, and the murder weapon, which was found near the scene of the crime, a six inch knife, was shown to the jury. Chindamo was convicted of murder and sentenced to be detained during Her Majesty's pleasure. A month later Christopher Gan was sentenced to three years' detention for his part in sparking off the feud that led to Philip Lawrence's death.

Perhaps we should leave the last word to the Catholic Archbishop of Westminster, Cardinal Basil Hume, quoting John 15:13: 'Greater love hath no man than this, that a man lay down his life for his friends.'

References

The Times

Supernatural Murder

The Norah Farnario Case

In *The Supernatural Murders* Jonathan Goodman defines the subject as killings sparked off by beliefs about an unearthly power, or brought to light (and sometimes solved) by transcendental means, or murders which give rise to legends or remind readers of old ones. But for many writers, and readers as well, the supernatural has a fascination because of its atmospheric and dramatic possibilities, and because the subject is a veritable goldmine of mystery stories.

The case of Norah Farnario (or Netta Fornario, as she is sometimes known) is a good example. When the body of a lightly clothed young woman was found after a freezing night on a bleak moor on the island of Iona, a local doctor put the death down to heart failure. She was buried in the cemetery on Iona with a plain headstone carrying the inscription *N.E.F. Died 19th November, 1929. Aged 33 years.*

But Norah was no ordinary islander. She had been found clothed in a robe that was the uniform of the Order of Alpha and Omega, an occult organisation with its headquarters in London. Clenched in her hand was a knife and beneath her body a cross had been roughly cut into the turf. She had come to the island from London a few weeks earlier and boarded with one of the crofters. She dressed in what would be known today as 'ethnic' clothing, wore exotic jewellery, wrote poetry and went for long solitary walks and was reckoned by the locals to be somewhat peculiar.

Near the end of her stay she became very agitated and told her hosts one Sunday that she must get off the island. But there was no ferry that day. She went to bed that night, but by the morning had disappeared, and her body was found the next day. The psychic world immediately said that she had been the victim of a psychic attack and though much has since been written about the death, it still remains the basis of much speculation.

There have been cases of psychic mediums assisting the police in difficult murder cases. One of the most well known operatives was

Peter Hurkos, a Dutch psychic detective, who developed his powers after a fall in 1941. Apparently by handling a person's belongings he could give information about the owner's personality, and was said to be responsible for solving a murder case in Miami in 1958.

But an interesting psychic case with a twist occurred in July 1928, near Edmonton, Canada. A farming family, mother, older son and two farm hands, were found shot to death. The youngest son, Vernon Booher, was strongly suspected of the crime, but the police could not find the murder weapon. They called on the services of a Dr Maximilian Langsner, who went to the farm and after casting about for some time soon pointed the waiting policemen to the location of the missing rifle. In addition he said he might be able to read the suspect's mind, and if Booher was thinking about the murder, Langsner would be able to give the police valuable information. After spending some time sitting on a chair outside Booher's cell and staring at him through the bars, the doctor withdrew and soon afterwards the farm worker confessed to the murders.

But at his trial Booher's counsel brought forward a unique defence. He claimed that his client had been under the hypnotic influence of Dr Langsner when he confessed and therefore the confession should be ruled invalid. The judge agreed and ruled that since Booher was a simple farm boy he might indeed have been influenced by the doctor and the confession was thrown out. But the prosecution had an ace up their sleeve. They brought to the stand the governor of the jail where Booher had been held as a material witness. He said that Booher had confessed to him even before Dr Langsner had been brought into the case. This confession was allowed to stand and Vernon Booher was convicted of four murders and hanged at Fort Saskatchewan Jail in 1929.

References

The Encyclopedia of Occult and Supernatural Murder by Brian Lane, Headline, 1995

The Supernatural Murders by Jonathan Goodman, Piatkus, 1992

Crime and the Occult by Paul Tabori, David & Charles, 1974

Norah Farnario case
Scottish Murder Stories by Molly Whittington-Egan, Neil Wilson
Publishing, 1998
Glasgow Bulletin

Vernon Booher case
The Limits of Detection by Douglas Wynn, Warner Books, 1992
Edmonton Journal

6

KILLER COUPLES

Martha Beck and Raymond Fernandez

Martha Beck was a very large lady. She weighed 20 stone (127 kilograms) in 1947, when she was twenty-seven, due to a pituitary-ovarian deficiency, which had also caused her to develop early and gave her a strong sexual appetite. But her gross appearance made it difficult for her to attract and form lasting relationships with men. She had married Alfred Beck at her home in Pensacola, Florida, in 1944, after having a child in California. But her marriage only lasted six months and while pregnant again she divorced her husband.

Martha took after her mother in that she exhibited a dominating personality, but she had an overwhelming desire for love and affection and in 1947 she wrote to a Lonely Hearts club in New York. She reported, quite correctly, that she had nursing qualifications and that she was the superintendent of a children's home. She also said that she had her own apartment, which was true, and that she was comfortably off, which was not. The letter was answered by Raymond Fernandez who sent a telegram to tell Martha of his imminent arrival in Pensacola.

Raymond was thirty-three and had been born in Hawaii of Spanish parents, but he was an American citizen. Apparently quite a normal young man until he was thirty-one, a hatch fell on his head when he was employed as a seaman and he suffered possible brain damage. After that he became interested in black magic and was convinced that he could influence people's minds from a distance, especially women as he too had a strong libido. He began a career of meeting women through Lonely Hearts clubs and decamping with their money when he could.

When he met Beck he wasn't impressed and when he found out that she did not have a lot of money he left rapidly for New York, writing that he had feelings of deep respect for her, but not love and their association could not continue. Martha was devastated. She had fallen in love and when she received his letter she put her head in the gas oven. (Gas in those days contained the lethal carbon monoxide.) But a neighbour rescued her and somehow her farewell letter to Raymond was sent to him.

Fernandez seems to have been stricken with remorse, for he invited her to New York. She promptly dumped her two children on her mother and arrived at Raymond's address. He was completely honest with her, admitting that he already had a wife living in Spain and that he made his money fleecing lonely women, but she seems to have accepted this and moved in with him.

The next year, after several other adventures with women, he went to see Mrs Myrtle Young who was forty and a widow from Arkansas. Even though Martha went with him as his sister-in-law, Mrs Young was captivated by the sophisticated Latin lover. They married in August 1948 and Beck went with them on their honeymoon to Chicago. But Myrtle soon became fed up with Martha always being there and a blazing row developed between the two women. Afterwards Mrs Young took a quantity of barbiturates. The pair then put her, in a state of near collapse, on a bus for Arkansas. During the journey she did in fact collapse and died shortly afterwards in hospital, the death being put down to 'cerebral haemorrhage'.

The next victim was a Mrs Janet Fay, 66, a widow from upstate New York. Fernandez corresponded with her after he and Beck had run out of the money they had managed to swindle out of Mrs Young. Mrs Fay was a devout Roman Catholic and Fernandez claimed to share her beliefs. She was completely taken in and began transferring money to him almost immediately. He had again taken Martha with him when he visited Mrs Fay and introduced her as his sister. The trio drove back to an apartment rented by Beck and Fernandez in Long Island. The two women shared a bed and rows soon began. After a particularly bad one Janet Fay stormed out of the bedroom shouting that she would not allow Martha to live with them after she and Raymond were married. She went into his bedroom and Martha followed and felled her with a blow to the head from a hammer. The next day they bought a large trunk, put the body in it, and buried it in the cellar of another house they rented in the Queens district of New York City.

On the same day that Mrs Fay died Raymond received a letter, in reply to one of his, from a Mrs Delphine Downing, a 41-year-old widow living in Grand Rapids, Michigan, with her two-year-old daughter Rainelle. Again the pair went to see her and were soon living in the widow's house. Raymond began sleeping with Delphine while Martha was left alone and miserable. It is not precisely clear what happened next, except that on Sunday, February 27th 1949, Beck gave Mrs Downing some pills to bring about an abortion. But they were sleeping pills. And when Delphine had gone into a deep sleep Martha persuaded Raymond to wrap a towel round the unfortunate woman's head and shoot her with her own late husband's revolver. They buried the body in the cellar and some days later Beck drowned the child in the washtub and together they buried her alongside her mother.

Almost as soon as they had finished two suspicious neighbours knocked on the front door. Beck and Fernandez put them off and went out to a drive-in movie. But when they returned the police arrived and they were arrested. Fernandez immediately confessed everything that had happened since he met Beck and later she too made a confession that differed only in some details from that of Fernandez.

The confessions made front page news all over the country and the New York police soon discovered the body of Mrs Janet Fay. What particularly outraged public opinion was the brutal killing of the small child. The state of Michigan did not have the death penalty, but New York did and the authorities in Michigan readily agreed to extradite the pair to New York to stand trial for the murder of Mrs Janet Fay.

In June 1949 both were tried together in the Bronx County courthouse. The trial lasted forty-four days and they were both convicted of first degree murder and sentenced to death. They were electrocuted on March 8th 1951.

Fernanadez had previously told psychiatrists that he was not in love with Beck and she had become very depressed when this was reported to her. But two hours before he was due to die he sent her a message: 'I would like to shout my love for you to the world.' Martha hugged the matron who told her and said: 'Now that I know Raymond loves me I can go to my death bursting with joy.'

References
Introduction to Murder by Wenzell Brown, Andrew Dakers Ltd., 1953
Murder Casebook, vol. 2, Part 29, Marshall Cavendish Ltd., 1990
New York Times.

Bonnie and Clyde

This pair belied the theory that criminals come from broken homes. Both Clyde Barrow and Bonnie Parker were very much attached to their parents, particularly their mothers, and made many very dangerous journeys to see them and their families when they were being pursued by the police.

Clyde was born in Telico, Texas, into an extremely poor family, the sixth of eight children. Because his parents couldn't support all their offspring, Clyde and his older sister Nell were farmed out to relatives for long periods. When he was twelve his father took the family to live in West Dallas. Clyde, with very little schooling and an almost total lack of discipline at home, was soon a member of a teenage gang who indulged in car theft and various kinds of robbery with violence. Chased by the police in October 1929 with his elder brother Buck in a stolen car, Clyde escaped but Buck was captured and sentenced to five years.

While on the run Clyde, who was then twenty, met Bonnie Parker, 19, hitherto a law-abiding young waitress in downtown Dallas, but within a month he was captured and in January 1930 sentenced to two years in jail. He persuaded Bonnie to smuggle a revolver in to him and with it escaped. He was caught a week later and sentenced to fourteen years, but paroled after two years.

The harsh regime at Hunstville prison undoubtedly hardened Clyde, who now formed his own gang with Bonnie and usually one or more teenage friends, exhibiting a willingness to shoot anyone who got in his way. He killed a man in a store robbery and gunned down another who tried to stop him stealing his car, and a few days later shot and killed a lawman when police surrounded one of the gang hideouts.

During one of their chases the stolen car became stuck in some mud and they abandoned it, trying to escape on foot. Bonnie was captured, but Clyde escaped. While in jail Bonnie composed the first of two long poems, *The Ballad of Suicide Sal*, which romanticised the notion of an outlaw and helped to make the pair famous. But after a few weeks in jail she was released for lack of evidence and rejoined Clyde.

They roamed the states of Texas, Oklahoma, Arkansas, Missouri and Iowa, stealing cars, holding up stores, garages and occasional banks, and although ambushed many times and chased by police even more times they managed to escape, mainly because of Clyde's dare-devil driving. He could drive at high speed continuously for more than eight hours at a stretch and his knowledge of the side roads and by-roads of the southern states was uncanny.

When Buck Barrow was released from prison in March 1933 (he was actually pardoned by a kind-hearted state governor) he joined Clyde and Bonnie where they were holed up in Joplin, Missouri, and took his newly wed wife Blanche along with him. But their idyll was soon shattered when neighbours became suspicious, having seen the men carrying guns into the house, and called the police. The house was soon surrounded, but the gang made yet another spectacular escape with guns blazing away on both sides and after they had departed two policemen lay dead in the street.

But their luck could not hold out forever. In June, Clyde, driving fast towards a bridge near Wellington,Texas, saw too late that the bridge was closed. He swerved the car which went off the road and turned over bursting into flames. Bonnie was trapped, but Clyde with the help of two farmers got her out. She was severely burned and

Clyde again had to shoot their way out when one of the farmers got in touch with the law because Clyde would not call a doctor.

Bonnie remained ill and in great pain for many weeks. The following month the gang camped near the town of Dexter, Iowa, in a public park. But a holidaymaker came across the campsite and saw a bloodstained car mat and some bloody bandages. Hearing about the fugitives on the radio, he went to the police. This time they came in force. Fifty policemen, National Guardsmen and local vigilantes surrounded the camp. A hail of bullets poured into it. Buck was hit several times and died later in hospital. Blanche was captured, but Clyde, Bonnie and another man escaped by swimming a river.

As Bonnie continued to improve, the gang attempted a more audacious crime. On a foggy morning in January 1934 they crept up on a work party from Eastam Prison Farm in Texas and freed five convicts. During the mêlée a guard was shot and killed. One of the escaped prisoners was Henry Methvin, a 21-year-old farm worker, who joined up with the gang.

On April 1st that year Clyde was asleep in a car near Grapevine, Texas, with Bonnie and Methvin when they were approached by two motorcycle patrolmen. Even though the policemen had not drawn their guns Methvin panicked and opened fire. Bonnie and Clyde joined in and soon the patrolmen lay groaning on the ground. A local farmer who had witnessed the incident claimed that Bonnie then got out of the car and laughed as she finished off the two men.

The public had been fascinated for months by the fugitive pair. Their exploits had captured the imagination of newspaper readers all over the country. One cartoon showed a bemused sheriff with Bonnie and Clyde diving in and out of rabbit holes around him. But now public opinion was beginning to turn against them. Certainly the authorities made a determined effort to catch them. The governor of the prison attacked by Bonnie and Clyde paid for his own private detective, a former Texas Ranger called Frank Hamer. He joined up with two Texas Rangers, Ted Hinton, a crack shot, and Bob Alcorn, who had been appointed by the Sheriff of Dallas to track down the fugitives. With other Rangers in two cars they began following the fugitives all over Texas.

They received information that the gang were on the road to Louisiana, and knowing that Methvin was with them they guessed that Bonnie and Clyde might be making for a farm which Methvin's father owned in hilly country near Shreeveport. An ideal spot in which to hole up. The Texas Rangers went to Shreeveport and the local police told them Bonnie and Clyde had indeed been seen in the town. The local sheriff showed the Rangers the only road which led to Methvin's father's farm and pointed out the best place for an ambush. The Rangers took their places.

It was hot and the mosquitoes bit them continuously. They had to lie there for three days until, early in the morning of the the third day, Irvin Methvin, Henry's father, came up in his truck. They stopped him, immobilised his truck and handcuffed him to a tree – an operation which was completely illegal. Five hours later the fugitives appeared in their tan Ford. Clyde was driving while Bonnie studied a road map. Clyde stopped when he saw the truck, but didn't get out. Next, a fusillade of shots rang out and the pair died with more than fifty bullets in each of their bodies.

There have been a number of books written about them and five films, many of which depict Bonnie as the stronger character and the instigator of many of their crimes. This hardly seems reasonable. Clyde had embarked on a life of crime before he had even met Bonnie and nearly all the killings were committed by him or his young associates. Bonnie was undoubtedly fascinated by criminals and outlaws and the life they led and particularly by Clyde. And he returned her regard. The love they had for each other was undoubtedly strong, but their affair was doomed from the start as, according to Bonnie's writings, they both knew.

References

The Strange History of Bonnie and Clyde by John Treherne, Jonathan Cape, 1984
Murder Casebook, vol. 4, Part 56, Marshall Cavendish, 1991

Ian Brady and Myra Hindley (the Moors Murder Case)

This case illustrates a fact that many crime writers are aware of, but often forget, and this is that murder, at least in this country, is very rare and it takes a special kind of person to do it. Seventeen-year-old David Smith, Brady thought, would easily be converted into a murderer. The boy had a troubled youth, but by the age of thirteen could physically beat his father – and had done so. By fifteen he was a heavy drinker and had a record of violence and housebreaking. Yet when he saw Brady, an older man to whom he looked up and admired, kill another seventeen-year-old he was revolted and went to the police.

Ian Brady was born in Glasgow in January 1938. He was adopted at three months and stayed with his adoptive parents until he was seventeen. By that time he had already been convicted several times for burglary and housebreaking, but the last court decided that instead of a custodial sentence Brady should be sent to live with his natural mother in Manchester. He was a taciturn loner, but a voracious reader, mainly of Nazi literature and the writings of de Sade.

His continued criminal activities resulted in his arrest in Manchester in January, 1956, for handling stolen lead and he was sent to Borstal for two years. He came out an embittered man (as Clyde Barrow had been), but he had learned book-keeping in jail and this enabled him, in February 1959, to obtain a stock clerk's position with Millwards, a soap-making factory in the Manchester suburb of Gorton. At Millwards he met Myra Hindley.

She was born in July 1942. On the arrival of her sister Maureen, when she was four, she went to live with her maternal grandmother in Bannock Street, Gorton. Her attendance at school was poor, but she was a clever girl and did well at English. She was engaged at seventeen but broke it off, then at eighteen she went to work at Millwards. Up until then she was apparently a normal teenager. She said afterwards that her father was a drunk who physically abused her mother and herself, if she was there, and this was why she lived with her grandmother. She had been born a Catholic, brought up a Protestant, but returned to Catholicism at sixteen.

According to her diary, she viewed Brady from afar, since he hardly spoke and seemed largely to ignore her, but her writings revealed secret longings for him. Eventually, in December 1961, he took her home after an office party and their affair, once begun, developed rapidly. They went to bed on only their second date.

Hindley became obsessed with Brady, allowing him to take over her life and even influence her thinking. He introduced her to the books he loved, Hitler's *Mein Kampf*, Dostoevsky's *Crime and Punishment* and the works of Nietzsche and de Sade. Together they decided to become master criminals, a notion Brady had cherished for a long time, and planned bank raids and other criminal activities in meticulous detail. In June 1963 Brady moved in with Hindley and her now semi-invalid granny at Bannock Street. The next month saw their first murder.

Pauline Reade was sixteen, lived two doors away from Maureen Hindley's boyfriend David Smith and just round the corner from Brady and Hindley, and she was known to them all. She disappeared on July 12th 1963 and her whereabouts were unknown until July 1987, when her remains were discovered on Saddleworth Moor, just off the A635 Holmfirth to Oldham road. Hindley said much later that Brady took Pauline on to the moor while she parked the car – she always drove because Brady could not – sexually assaulted Pauline and cut her throat, burying the body in a shallow grave. Hindley afterwards posed for a photograph near the grave.

John Kilbride was next. He was twelve, and vanished from Ashton market, where Hindley used to shop, on November 23rd 1963. When Brady was arrested John's name was found in some notes he had made, and a photograph of Hindley standing on his moorland grave gave away his resting place.

Early in 1964 Brady, Hindley and her grandmother moved to Wardlebrook Avenue in Hattersely, just beyond Hyde, on the outskirts of Manchester. On June 16th that year twelve year old Keith Bennett left his home in Chorlton-upon-Medlock to visit his grandmother who lived half a mile away. He never arrived and his body has never been discovered. Brady confessed in 1987 that they gave him a lift and subsequently murdered him.

A search of the Wardlebrook Avenue house by the police after the arrest of Brady and Hindley brought to light a prayer book in the spine of which were found two tickets for the left luggage lockers at Manchester Central Station. The police retrieved two suitcases and in one was an audio tape. On it the terrified voice of ten-year-old Lesley Anne Downey could be heard, pleading with Brady and Hindley – their voices were both on the tape – not to undress and molest her. She was murdered at Wardlebrook Avenue on Boxing Day 1964, and her body recovered from a grave near Pauline Reade's. It was this tape, however, which so shocked the public that even today the prospect of Hindley's release raises anger in many people's minds.

The previous August, David Smith and Maureen Hindley had got married and they soon formed a foursome with Brady and Hindley. On October 6th 1965 Hindley drove Brady to Manchester Central Station where they picked up seventeen-year-old Eddie Evans, a young homosexual whom Brady knew. They drove him to Wardlebrook Avenue. Hindley then went to see her sister Maureen and asked David to walk her home. When they reached the Wardlebrook Avenue house she invited David in and put him in the kitchen. Then he heard her call out: 'Dave, help him, help him!' He rushed into the living room to find Evans lying on the settee and Brady hitting him on the head with an axe. When the poor youth was dead Brady and Hindley cleaned up the mess and Smith helped carry the body upstairs in a blanket.

When Smith got back home he was physically sick and after talking it over with Maureen called the police. The police waited until daylight to swoop on the Wardlebrook Avenue house, but they soon found the body upstairs. The investigation of the other murders was difficult and had to be pieced together from scraps of evidence culled from the notes Brady had made and photographs of Hindley on the moors near the burial sites. The pair denied everything and continued to do so at their Chester Assizes trial in April, 1966. But David Smith gave evidence against them and Brady was convicted of murdering Edward Evans, Lesley Anne Downey and John Kildbride. Hindley was found guilty of the murders of Evans and Downey and of being an accessory after the fact in the case of John Kilbride.

The murders of Pauline Reade and Keith Bennett were not finally solved until 1986/7, although the police strongly suspected Brady and Hindley of being involved. It was then that they both confessed and Hindley helped to find Reade's buried body on the moor. But neither of them could find the burial place of young Keith Bennett.

Interest in the case has surfaced again over Hindley's attempts to be released. Discussion of whether she should or should not is outside the scope of this book, but what is not is the relationship between them during the time of the murders. Brady was undoubtedly the dominant personality and it was his ideas that Hindley followed, but what happened, as probably nearly always happens with killer couples, was that through Hindley's support and encouragement Brady scaled heights of evil which he probably wouldn't have reached on his own. The combination of the two personalities pushed their actions to an extreme rarely found between men and women.

References

The Moors Murders by David Marchbanks, Frewin, 1966

The Monsters of the Moors by John Dean Potter, Elek, 1966

Beyond Belief by Emlyn Williams, Hamish Hamilton, 1967

On Iniquity by Pamela Hansford Johnson, Macmillan, 1967

Devil's Disciples by Robert Wilson, Express Newspapers, 1986

Topping by Peter Topping with Jean Ritchie, Angus & Robertson, 1989 (Detective Chief Superintendent Peter Topping was the policeman in charge of the reopening of the Moors Murder case in 1986)

Pauline Parker and Juliet Hulme

Pauline Parker was sixteen and Juliet Hulme just fifteen when together they murdered Pauline's mother. Not only that but they had been planning it for weeks beforehand. In Pauline's diary she had written: 'I am trying to think of some way' [to murder her mother.] 'I want it to appear a natural or an accidental death.' And later: 'We discussed the "moider" fully, so next time I write in the diary Mother will be dead. How odd, yet how pleasing.' And for June 22nd 1954 there was only one line. 'The day of the happy event.'

Yet these were two intelligent girls who had had a good education and came from apparently caring families. But both had experienced lonely childhoods, each of them finding it difficult to make friends, and Pauline in particular had a strong stubborn streak. When they met, a strong emotional bond formed between them.

Juliet Hulme was born in England, but came to New Zealand with her family who emigrated when she was nine. Her father became the Rector of Canterbury University College in Christchurch and Juliet went to the Girls High School. There she met Pauline Parker who had been born and brought up in Christchurch.

They became firm friends and soon Pauline was spending all her spare time with Juliet in the latter's palatial home in the suburbs of Christchurch. They invented their own private world and filled it with their own invented characters, both of them writing stories about it. When they could, they bathed together and slept together.

But their parents became worried by the relationship. Juliet's father even considered having his daughter psychoanalysed, but was advised that she was too young for that. Eventually he accepted an appointment in England and on the way back proposed to send Juliet to school in South Africa. Pauline pleaded to be able to go too, but both sets of parents were adamant that the girls must be separated and the date for the departure was fixed for July 3rd 1954.

On June 22nd the two young women persuaded Mrs Parker to take them for a farewell picnic in Victoria Park, Christchurch. The two girls carried with them an unusual pink stone and a brick wrapped in a stocking. When they had had their meal Juliet went ahead up the path and unobtrusively dropped the pink stone. The other two followed and Pauline pointed the stone out to her mother who stooped to examine it. Pauline Parker swung the brick in the stocking.

It took more than forty blows to kill the poor woman and by now the carefully worked out plan of saying that Mrs Parker had fallen and hit her head on a brick was in tatters. But they went ahead with it, rushing into a nearby tea room to call for help. When the body was examined, however, it was obvious that Mrs Parker had been attacked and Pauline and Juliet soon confessed to the police.

They were tried for murder at the Supreme Court in Christchurch in August 1954. The defence pleaded insanity and a psychiatrist referred to the girls as suffering from *folie à deux*, a term sometimes used to describe a kind of communicated insanity, although there is no academic acceptance of the idea. But the prosecution would have none of this. They brought their own psychiatrists to show that the girls were not insane. One of them reported that Juliet said: 'You would have to be an absolute moron not to know that murder was against the law,' which proves that in law Juliet was sane, but goes nowhere to explain her mental state.

They were both convicted of murder and sentenced to be detained during Her Majesty's pleasure, the only sentence which could be passed on persons under eighteen convicted of a crime punishable by death. They were sent to prisons 400 miles apart. Both were model prisoners and Pauline passed her school certificate in prison. They received psychiatric treatment and were released on parole in November 1959.

Both suffered from the fact that a lesbian relationship was looked upon in those days with fear and loathing and the efforts made by their parents to break it up probably only served to strengthen it. But their relationship shows the effects of a strong emotional drive linked to the combination of two personalities that together magnified the worst aspects of both. Separately each of them might not have done much harm to anyone, but together they became lethal.

References

Christchurch Star

Murder Casebook, vol.2, Part 28, Marshall Cavendish, 1990

Real-Life Crimes, vol .7, Part 100, Eaglemoss Publications Ltd., 1994

Fred and Rosemary West

For sheer horror, this case rivals the Moors Murders. But whereas Brady and Hindley tortured and killed young children and the Wests older teenagers, the sheer number of the Wests', in particular Fred West's crimes must put them among the most evil people in this century in this country.

The thing that undoubtedly cemented the relationship between this couple was sex. Frederick West had been sexually abused by both his father and mother as a child and he in his turn carried the outrage into his own family, having sexual intercourse with his daughters on a regular basis until they left home. Rosemary had an incestuous relationship with her father which lasted until she was sixteen, when she moved in with Fred. Both were obsessed with sex. West had to leave home when he was nineteen for making a thirteen-year-old girl pregnant. He was charged by the police with having unlawful sex, but the case was subsequently dropped. Rose, according to her brother, when she was only fifteen regularly had sex with lorry drivers at a roadside snack bar where she worked.

West was born in 1941 near the Herefordshire village of Much Marcle. In 1962 he married Catherine (Rena) Costello, a Scottish teenager and part-time prostitute and they went to live in Rena's home at Coatbridge, now almost an outer suburb of Glasgow. But three years later they moved back to Herefordshire. They had two children by this time, although Fred was not the natural father of the elder, Charmaine. Two local teenaged girls decided to go with them after Fred had painted a glowing picture of the job situation in England. One of them, Anne McFall, became infatuated with him, and when the marriage became distinctly rocky, and Rena went back to Scotland, Anne McFall stayed on with West and the two young children in the small caravan near the village of Kempley, twelve miles from Gloucester.

Late in 1966 Anne became pregnant by West, but by the next year she had disappeared. He gave out that she had returned to Glasgow, but her remains were recovered, twenty years later, from a field near

Kempley, together with her unborn child. This could have been his first murder, although several teenaged girls had disappeared in Glasgow at about the time he lived there. But although he led the police to her grave he always denied being involved in her death. And the reason for it remains a mystery.

Rena returned to live with Fred at intervals, but in early 1969 he met the fifteen-year-old Rosemary Letts and a year later she went to live with him in a caravan at Bishop's Cleeve, near Cheltenham. Undoubtedly she was flattered by the attentions of a man who was twelve years older than she, but the major attraction was undoubtedly sex and a year later she gave birth to her first child, Heather. They were now living at 25 Midland Road, Gloucester.

The same year West was convicted of theft and sent to prison for twelve months. It was said at Rosemary West's trial that it was during this period that Charmaine, who didn't like Rose and wanted to return to her own mother, disappeared. Her remains were discovered, also about twenty years later, under the kitchen floor at Midland Road. The body had been dismembered, just like all the others, and West undoubtedly buried her. But whether he actually killed her is open to doubt.

It appears that around this time Rena also disappeared. In fact West said that he killed them both on the same day, but this is unlikely, since he was obviously trying to protect Rose when he made the confession. But it was to be many years before the full story finally came out.

In August 1992, when the family were living at 25 Cromwell Street, Gloucester, one of West's younger daughters complained to Rose that he had raped her forcibly and hurt her, while her mother was out shopping. 'Oh well,' said Rose. 'You were asking for it.' But when he continued to have sexual relations with the girl and even recorded it on video, she told a schoolfriend about it. The friend told her parents who got in touch with the police.

The Gloucester police, in particular Detective Constable Hazel Savage, had been hearing rumours about incest in the West household for some time. She began interviewing the family and friends and discovered that the Wests had been charged with a sexual assault back in 1973.

Seventeen-year-old Caroline Owens had been the Wests' nanny for some time, but left because she disliked Fred and felt that Rose was showing too much interest in her sexually. One night in December 1972 she said goodbye to her boyfriend in Tewksbury and was later offered a lift home in the Wests' car. Rose sat in the back with her and soon began kissing her and caressing her breasts. She protested and Fred stopped the car, leaned over the front seat and began punching her until she passed out. When she came to, her hands were tied behind her back and Fred was taping her mouth. She was taken to Cromwell Street and in an upstairs room she was stripped and molested by Rose, raped by her and later by Fred. He told her if she wasn't careful he would kill her and bury her under the paving stones of Gloucester. The next day after further molestation and being raped again she escaped by promising to come back as the Wests' nanny. She felt too ashamed to say anything when she returned home, but her mother saw the bruises on her and told the police. But Caroline could not face going to court and repeating details of the rapes so the Wests were only charged with indecent assault and fined £50.

History repeated itself in 1992. An older daughter of the Wests had suffered being held down by her mother while her father raped her on a periodic basis from when she was eight and she had run away from home when she was fifteen. She had been persuaded by the police to give evidence to corroborate the younger daughter's story. But when the case came to court none of the children would testify against their parents and the Wests again escaped justice.

During the police investigations, however, DC Hazel Savage heard rumours of another missing girl, Rose's eldest child, Heather. She had disappeared in 1987, when she was seventeen, and the Wests gave out that she had gone to work in a holiday camp in Devon. She never came back and some of the West children actually went to the holiday camp to look for her, but the owners had never heard of Heather. And then one of the younger West children, who had been taken into care, told her foster parents that her father had said that if they were not good children they would end up under the patio like their sister Heather. But the children had always thought their father was joking.

DC Hazel Savage began a systematic search through records for Heather, but no trace of her could be found after 1987. She badgered her superiors to search the back garden of 25 Cromwell Road and eventually her persistence paid off. On February 23rd 1994 the police obtained search warrants and began to dig up the back garden.

Fred went down to the police station to protest, but then seemed to have a change of mind. He said that Heather was buried there, although the police were looking in the wrong place. West explained that Heather had died accidentally and he had buried her in a panic. The police eventually unearthed the remains and they were examined by the eminent pathologist Professor Bernard Knight. But he found more thigh bones than he should have. Clearly there was more than one body buried there. When told about this, West said that there were two more bodies buried at Cromwell Street. Further questioning soon elicited what West said was a full confession. He admitted to nine more killings, bringing the total to twelve, including Rena and Anne McFall, who had been buried in neighbouring fields at Kempley, and his step-daughter Charmaine who had been buried at 25 Midland Road.

Examination of the bones showed the bodies had all been dismembered and many had been buried with some sort of restraint, either belts or ropes. Some of the skulls still had tape around them and in some cases metal tubes had been inserted, presumably into the nose, so that the victim could be gagged to prevent them calling out and yet kept alive. This raised the dreadful spectre of torture. It certainly looked as if the Wests not only sexually abused their victims before killing them but possibly tortured them as well.

The police actually managed to trace the identities of all eight of the non-West victims. They were all young girls who had either worked for the family, lodged at 25 Cromwell Street, or had been kidnapped by the Wests after having been offered lifts in their car.

Fred West actually admitted all the murders and claimed that Rose had not been involved in any of them. And Rose concurred. She said that Fred had sent her out to work as a prostitute when he was presumably murdering the girls. But Rose had a room in 25 Cromwell Street specially equipped for prostitution, with hardcore videos and magazines to hand and equipment for bondage and sadomasochistic practices. She regularly offered her services in contact magazines.

At the committal proceedings she would not look at Fred and shrank away when he tried to touch her. She was reported in the press as saying that she hated him. Fred seemed to become increasingly depressed either from this, the prospect of never getting out of jail or possibly remorse for the suffering he had caused, or a combination of all three, and on New Year's Day 1995 he hanged himself in his cell at Winson Green Prison, Birmingham.

But the trial of Rose West went ahead at Winchester Crown Court in October 1995. The evidence against her was purely circumstantial, but then it is in many murder trials. But the evidence of Caroline Owens and some of her own children who recalled how she had participated in the sexual abuse of them went against her. In addition a number of witnesses testified to Charmaine having disappeared while Fred was still in prison, which seemed to indicate that she had been involved in at least one murder on her own.

The jury eventually brought in a verdict of guilty of ten murders, and the judge said that if attention was paid to what he recommended she would never be released from prison.

References
Fred and Rose by Howard Sounes, Warner Books, 1995
'She Must Have Known' by Brian Masters, 1996 (In this book Masters makes the case that Rose West should not have been convicted)
Murder in Mind, 1, Marshall Cavendish, 1996

7

CRIMES AGAINST THE PERSON

Blackmail

It has always seemed to me that crime novels, where the blackmailer is murdered because he or she has pushed the victim too far, overstate the case. I would have thought that hardly any blackmailer would be foolish enough to disturb the goose that lays the golden eggs. In a recent case a shy bank manager reportedly gave a blackmailer nearly £500,000 over twenty years. He sold his big house for a smaller one, remortgaged that, cashed in his and his wife's investments and borrowed heavily from friends, but all that happened in the end was that in deperation he went to the police. Another intriguing story concerned a murder which happened in Hollywood in the 1920s.

William Desmond Taylor was a famous Hollywood director of the silent era. Born in Ireland in 1867, by 1922 he had starred in several Hollywood films, but had turned to directing as he grew too old for playing romantic leads. Early on the morning of February 2nd his valet/butler, who did not live in, found his body lying on the living-room floor when he arrived for work. He called in neighbours and the studios and by the time the police arrived the house was full of people and evidence of Taylor's numerous affairs with actresses, and indeed anything the studios considered controversial, had been removed almost by the cartload.

At first it was thought that he had died of natural causes, but when the coroner arrived and the body was moved it was discovered that he had been shot in the back. Speculation and rumours abounded in the press. It was known that he had been associating with the Hollywood silent film star Mabel Normand, who was 23 years old and had made sixteen films since 1916, but whose career was now on the wane, and Mary Miles Minter, 20, who was being groomed to replace Mary Pickford as 'America's Sweetheart'.

Neighbours had heard a shot at 7.45 the previous night, just after Mabel Normand, who had called to see Taylor, had left. There was ample evidence that Mary Miles Minter was in love with the director, but she had an alibi. She was reading to her whole family – her sister, mother and grandmother – at home at the time. The police questioned hundreds of witnesses but made no arrests. Nevertheless persistent rumours linked Mary Miles Minter and her mother, Charlotte Selby, with the crime.

Charlotte Selby was perhaps one of the most obnoxious of the Hollywood mothers. She took complete control of both her daughters' stage and film careers, kept them short of money and refused to allow the girls to live lives of their own. It was known that she owned a Smith and Wesson 0.38 calibre pistol (the same calibre as the bullet which killed Taylor) and had threatened several of her daughters' would-be suitors with it. Several strands of Mary's hair were also found on Taylor's jacket. But the District Attorney of Los Angeles took no action against Charlotte or Mary.

In 1926 a new District Attorney, Asa Keyes, was appointed and he reopened the case. He found that Charlotte had not been listening to her daughter reading on the night of the murder. But Charlotte then produced two witnesses, a friend, Carl Stockdale, and a night-watchman, who gave her an alibi for the time of the murder. Yet again, nothing was done.

In 1937 with yet another District Attorney at Los Angeles, Buron Fitts, Charlotte and Mary applied to him to produce any evidence he had linking them with the crime or to publicly exonerate them. This he did and the case still remains officially unsolved.

Then in 1983 a young American writer, Sidney Kirkpatrick, wanted to write a biography of the famous 1920s film director King Vidor. He unearthed a cache of material on the Taylor case, which Vidor had collected in 1967, presumably intending to write a screen-play about the murder. The material which Vidor collected strongly suggested that Charlotte Selby had indeed been the murderer. She had been obsessed with breaking up the affair between Mary and Taylor and on the night of the murder had locked Mary in her room. But

Mary's grandmother released her and Mary went straight to Taylor's house. When Mabel Normand arrived she hid upstairs in a bedroom. Later Taylor escorted Mabel to her car and Charlotte, who had been searching for Mary, slipped inside the house. As Taylor re-entered the living room and Mary came down the stairs Charlotte shot him in the back.

The evidence which Vidor collected suggested that all three Los Angeles District Attorneys had known the truth and each had blackmailed Charlotte. They had forced her to pay out something like $750,000, a very large sum for those days, over a period of fifteen years, although Buron Fitts apparently destroyed the evidence the police had against Mary and Charlotte in return for a one-off payment. There was also evidence that Charlotte had paid Carl Stockdale for giving her an alibi. All this came to light because the girls finally rebelled against their mother and sued her in the courts for money which they said she had siphoned off from their estates in order to pay off her blackmailers.

References

A Cast Of Killers by Sidney Kirkpatrick, Hutchinson, 1986
Los Angeles Times

Bombing

In recent years a series of bombings has occurred in America and Europe, perpetrated by people unconnected with regular terrorist groups. An example is Theodore Kaczynski, who to crime writers might be thought to epitomise the mad scientist or master criminal, a super-intelligent individual who for some reason goes off the rails and devotes his life to crime. But in reality this was more likely to be the sad case of a brilliant man who suffered mental instability.

A parcel bomb was sent to the Northwestern University, Illinois, on May 26th 1978 causing severe injuries to the person who opened it. In the following seventeen years there were a further fifteen separate attacks. They were all letter or parcel bombs and were sent mainly to universities, airline offices and computer installations or to individuals who worked in these places. And thus the criminal acquired the name 'Unabomber'. Among many other devastating and crippling injuries suffered by the victims, a professor at the University of California, at Berkeley, lost his right eye and hand, and three people actually died. A computer store owner in Salt Lake City was killed by a parcel bomb left outside his shop, an advertising executive succumbed to his injuries in Caldwell, New Jersey, and a well-known advocate of timber felling was blown up in an office in Sacramento, California.

The FBI – since this was a case covering several states it was handled by the FBI – had very few clues as to who the bomber might be. The consensus of opinion seemed to be that he was a mad professor who lived somewhere in Northern California. In June 1995, however, he made his first mistake. Emboldened possibly by the publicity he had received, he sent a 35,000 word 'manifesto' to the *New York Times* and the *Washington Post,* with the threat that unless it was published by at least one of the newspapers he would send a bomb to an unspecified destination 'with intent to kill'. The Attorney General of the USA and the Director of the FBI both recommended publication, but the newspaper editors agonised for weeks and when finally they did publish it, in September 1995, the decision was greeted by a storm of derision from the media. The editors were accused of turning the bomber into a national celebrity and sending a message to other terrorists that America gives in to threats.

But the ploy worked. The manifesto was a verbose diatribe against technology and the industrialised society, but the rhetoric struck a chord with one man. He was David Kaczynski, 46, a social worker in New York and in turning out the attic of his mother's home he had come across some papers containing writings very similar to the rantings of the Unabomber in his manifesto.

The writings were from his older brother Ted. Theodor Kaczynski had been a brilliant mathematician, studying at the University of Michigan and at Harvard where he obtained a PhD, becoming a university professor in Berkeley. But in 1969 he abruptly resigned his position and took a series of menial jobs around northern California and Utah. Then he bought some land in the Bitteroot Mountains, near Lincoln in Montana, built himself a shack and lived there as a hermit.

He corresponded with his family occasionally and when David found the writings in the attic he wrote asking if he could visit his brother, but Ted refused. This made David doubly suspicious and after much heart searching he eventually got in touch with the FBI. Agents surrounded the primitive cabin in the woods and Theodore Kaczynski was arrested without trouble.

Inside the shack was found a large quantity of bomb making materials, and explosives manuals in both English and Spanish, which Kaczynski spoke fluently. Two typewriters were also taken away to see if the manifesto had been typed on either.

Kaczynski was brought to trial in Sacramento in January 1998, charged with causing the deaths of three people and injuries to twenty-nine. But immediately he posed the legal system a problem. His lawyers wanted him to plead insanity, since there was a wealth of evidence against him and he had no hope of being found not guilty, but he refused and wanted to dismiss them. His lawyers then claimed that his insanity was such that he could not bear to be described as insane and thus could not co-operate in his own defence. And just before the trial started he tried to commit suicide in his cell by hanging himself with his underwear. Eventually the situation was resolved when Kaczynski pleaded guilty to all charges and the prosecution agreed not to ask for the death penalty. He was given a life sentence without possibility of parole. The million dollar reward offered by the FBI for help in bringing the Unabomber to justice was given, in August 1998, to David Kaczynski. He said he would give the money to the victims and their families.

References

The Times
The New York Times

Gangsters

According to Claire Sterling in her book *Crime without Frontiers* the collapse of communism in Russia and the fragmentation of the Soviet empire left a large void in the forces of law and order, which was rapidly filled by lawless elements. This has led to the linking up of crime groups in America and Europe, trafficking mainly in drugs and illegal arms, to form a loose confederation of mafias. There have been reports of summit meetings in Warsaw, Prague and Berlin. So the time may not be far off, if we haven't already reached it, when the world crime scene is dominated by Mafia-like groups. And though this must be an appalling situation for law enforcement agencies, and the rest of us, it offers a wealth of material for crime writers.

A simple story, which nevertheless illustrates the essential barbarity of organised crime – even on a small scale – began during the afternoon of August 6th 1997 in Bolton, Lancashire. John Bates, 28, was walking along a street in the Deane district of the city, hand in hand with his stepson, five-year-old Dillon Hull, when he was approached by a man wearing a crash-helmet with a full-face visor. The man produced a gun and opened fire. Bates turned and started running, but felt a bullet enter his side. His stepson let go of his hand and he turned to see the little boy lying in the road. He had been shot twice in the back of the head, and died on the way to hospital. The gunman dived down an alleyway, abandoning his crash helmet and also leaving behind an old yellow Metro.

John Bates was soon out of hospital and interviewed by the police. He admitted being a drug dealer, claiming that he dealt in heroin to support his own addiction, which cost him £50 per day. He had been living with Dillon's mother for several years, although Dillon's natural father was a Manchester Rastafarian, who had left soon after Dillon was born. Bates and Dillon's mother had previously lived in Blackburn, where he had also dealt in drugs, and they had only been living in Bolton for a few weeks.

Bates said that he had come into conflict with a local drug supplying gang. He had been invited to a local pub where he had met several dealers and drug suppliers. He was told that he was undercutting them and was then offered a deal by one of the drug suppliers present – go back to Blackburn and begin dealing there from his new supplier. Bates said he would think it over, but subsequently rejected the offer and said he would quit dealing in drugs altogether. But by this time he was under sentence of death. And shots were fired through the window of the house he occupied with Dillon's mother, narrowly missing the family.

On October 9th 1998 at Preston Crown Court, Paul Seddon was accused of murdering Dillon Hull and attempting to murder John Bates. Seddon's fingerprints had been found both on the crash helmet and the yellow Metro and he had been identified by Bates and two other witnesses as the gunman. David Hargreaves, 24, and Craig Hollinrake, 25, were charged together with another Bolton man with conspiracy to murder.

The original plan had been for Seddon to buy the Metro at a local scrapyard and drive to where Bates lived. Hollinrake was to arrive by taxi and try to lure the victim outside his front door so that Seddon could shoot him. But when he got there he found that Bates had been sent by Dillon's mother to find him and bring him home. The gunman waited for his quarry to return. He was subsequently convicted of murder, the judge recommending that he should serve at least twenty-five years. Hargreaves was sentenced to eighteen and Hollinrake sixteen years and the fourth man was acquitted.

References

Crime without Frontiers by Claire Sterling, Little, Brown, 1994
Gangland, vols. 1 and 2, by James Morton, Little, Brown, 1992, 1994
World Encyclopedia of Organised Crime by Jay Robert Nash, Paragon House, 1992
Tough Jews by Rich Cohen, Jonathan Cape, 1998
Blackburn Citizen
Bolton Evening News

Kidnapping

A brief overview of kidnapping, including motives for the crime, is given in the *Crime Writer's Handbook*. From the point of view of the fiction writer the major interest will probably be in the mechanism of the kidnap plot: how and where the victim is held, communication about the ransom, payment of the ransom, the release of the victim and the tracking down of the perpetrators of the crime. Sometimes, of course, the victim might be murdered to prevent him or her giving information about where they were held, and so on.

Kidnapping is quite common. Even in England there were 250 kidnappings in the metropolitan area in 1995, although this includes short-term abductions where men forcibly take away women for sexual interference or rape and release the victim afterwards. Political kidnapping (hostage taking) is common in many parts of the world and kidnapping for money prevalent in very poor countries.

In the late 1970s and early 1980s kidnapping was very common in Italy. A typical case involved the managing director of the Rome branch of a multinational company. Leaving a motorway one evening on the way home he found the slipway blocked by a car. He tried to back up but a vehicle came up behind him. The gang smashed the windows of his car, dragged him out and bundled him into the car in front, which then sped off.

He was held in a small cubby-hole, about six feet long by three or four feet wide and high, which led off a garage in what appeared to be a remote house which the gang occupied. He was held in those cramped conditions for nearly five months until the ransom was paid.

Initially the kidnappers demanded the equivalent of £5 million, an astronomical sum for those days, but the man's wife employed a British kidnap consultant who gave her advice on how to handle the negotiations and the final figure was brought down to the equivalent of £400,000. It still represented the bulk of their life savings, but it gained the release of the husband. And the kidnappers were never apprehended. In some cases if the negotiations took too long the kidnapping gangs might lose patience and kill the victim or cut off fingers or ears to send to his family.

A bizarre case occurred in London in 1996. A Chinese chef who had not long been in this country and could speak no English was kidnapped by Chinese criminals. He was held in a house in north London, handcuffed to a radiator, while his nineteen year old wife was phoned in China. She was forced to listen to the screams of her husband who was being beaten up in London. Initially the ransom was the equivalent of £40,000 to be paid in China, but eventually it was negotiated down to £12,000. The wife's family contacted the Chinese police who got in touch with the Metropolitan Police. There was a remarkable liaison between the two police forces, even though there was time delay in communications and the British police had to use a Mandarin translator. Two British policemen went to China, since, using a dialect the kidnappers did not understand, the victim in London was able to send messages to his wife. Eventually the location of the kidnap house was found.

When the ransom was finally handed over in China the Chinese police arrested the receivers of the money. At the same time the house in north London was raided and the hostage released.

References
The Kidnap Business by Mark Bles and Robert Low, W. H. Allen, 1987
The Times

Rape

In early December 1985 a small red-haired Irishman appeared at a West Hendon magistrates court to answer bail. He had been charged some weeks earlier with assaulting his estranged wife and her boyfriend and also raping her. Into the back of the court came a police detective with a twenty-year-old woman. She had previously been raped in Copthal Park, north London, and the detective wondered if she would recognise the Irishman as the man who sexually assaulted her. But she couldn't. The small man, however, whose name was John Duffy, recognised her, as he had indeed raped her. And he realised that he was in grave danger of being recognised by a rape victim. It was this which launched him on his career of murder.

His series of rapes had begun in June 1982, when he and another man pounced on a young woman coming out of Hampstead railway station in north-west London, dragged her to some waste ground and raped her. This was followed by five attacks in the next few weeks and during the subsequent twelve months eighteen young women were raped by the pair. All the attacks were close to railway stations which Duffy knew well as he had been employed as a carpenter by British Rail. And he later became known as the Railway Rapist.

There was then a gap, afterwards put down to the fact that the little Irishman had been reunited with his wife. They had previously parted because of rows over not being able to have children. Duffy blamed his wife, but in fact it was he who had a very low sperm count. He also had rape fantasies and liked to tie up his wife before sex. But their reconciliation was short lived and soon they parted again. Duffy went back to haunting railway stations, and the ill-lit footpaths and car parks near them, looking for young women on their way home, this time on his own.

Early in 1984 he attacked and raped a woman at knife point on Barnes Common and the assaults continued mostly in west and north-west London. By July 1985, when he raped three women in one night in the Hampstead and Hendon areas, the police were beginning to realise that one man was responsible for all the rapes. A task force, called Operation Hart, was put together to track him down. But by the end of the year Duffy's activities were to escalate dramatically.

On December 29th 1985 nineteen-year-old secretary Alison Day left her Hornchurch home to travel to Hackney in east London by rail to meet her boyfriend who worked in a factory there. Her body was found seventeen days later at the bottom of a canal near Hackney Wick station. Her hands were tied behind her back with some special industrial string and she had been raped and strangled with a strip of her skirt fastened round her neck and tightened with a small piece of wood inserted into the loop of material and turned.

Four months later, fifteen-year-old Dutch school girl Maartje Tamboezer was riding her cycle along a footpath by the side of the London railway line near East Horsley in Surrey when she was thrown from the vehicle by a piece of rope tied across the footpath. Her body was found the next day. She had been tied like Alison Day, raped and strangled in the same way and her body set on fire to try and remove forensic evidence.

In May, a 29-year-old newly married secretary at London Weekend Television, Anne Lock, disappeared from Brookman's Park station at 10 o'clock at night. Her body was not found for nine weeks. Then it was discovered near an overgrown railway embankment. But by that time decomposition made it very difficult to determine the circumstances of her death. Nevertheless it appeared that she been killed and maltreated like the others.

The day before Anne Lock vanished, Duffy was arrested at North Weald railway station for loitering in a suspicious manner and was found to be be carrying a knife, but the local police, not knowing his previous history, let him go. The disappearance of the television secretary finally galvanised the police from London, Surrey and Hertfordshire into action. They combined in a new operation. Five thousand sex offenders were investigated and Duffy, because of the rape of his wife, was on the list. He was called in for questioning in July, but arrived with a solicitor and refused to give a blood sample. Later he was admitted to a psychiatric hospital suffering from what he said was loss of memory and could not be questioned further by the police. But Duffy was only a part-time patient.

In the summer of that year the head of Operation Hart had asked the Professor of Applied Psychology at Surrey University, David Canter, for help. Using a system developed by the American FBI called Psychological Offender Profiling he was able to develop a profile of the Railway Rapist, listing seventeen pointers to the character of the criminal. These were fed into a computer which came up with John Duffy's name; thirteen of the pointers fitted Duffy exactly.

The police began a round-the-clock surveillance of his home in Kilburn and began tailing him. He was arrested in November 1986. In his mother's house was found a ball of string identical to the material used to tie up all the killer's victims, and fibres found on Alison Day's clothes matched those from one of his pullovers.

John Duffy was tried at the Old Bailey in February 1987 on only five counts of rape, since many of his rape victims could not stand the trauma of giving evidence in court, and the three murders. He was convicted of four rapes and the murders of Alison Day and Maartje Tamboezer, since in the case of Anne Lock there was little forensic evidence. Nevertheless the police still strongly believe that he killed her. He was sentenced to life with the proviso that he should serve at least thirty years.

References

Criminal Shadows by David Canter, HarperCollins, 1994

Real-Life Crimes, vol.1, Part 1, Eaglemoss Publications Ltd., 1993

Murder Casebook, vol.5, Part 75, Marshall Cavendish, 1991

8

VILLAINY UNLIMITED

Arson

Arson provides a wealth of stories for crime writers, because of the number of reasons one can have for the crime. The deliberate setting fire to property is often done for commercial reasons, to collect on the insurance (a crime which tends to rise as the economic state of an area declines) but this is dealt with elsewhere in this book. The fire can be set for revenge. The Spanish Club was a Soho drinking dive in 1980. A customer, thinking he had been overcharged for a drink, returned with a can and poured petrol through the letter box. In the ensuing fire thirty-seven people died. Another purpose for setting fires is for sexual excitement. It is considered to be an attribute of some serial killers. The Son of Sam serial killer is said to have started some 2000 fires in and around New York before he graduated to shooting courting couples, and Peter Kurten, the Dusseldorf sadist who operated between 1929 and 1931, wrote that watching a big fire he had set – especially if it involved people being killed – always gave him an orgasm. But some of the most interesting and involved stories concern killers who use a fire to conceal the identity of a victim.

On the night of July 30th 1925 an explosion rocked the little town of Walnut Creek, near San Francisco. There was a fire at the small chemical plant near the town and when the fire brigade had put out the flames they discovered the body of a man in the ashes. His wife identified him, by his watch and some jewellery found on the body, as Charles Schwartz, the proprietor of the chemical works who had stayed late at the plant to continue his research into a secret process for the manufacture of artificial silk. The identification was confirmed by the local doctor, who knew Schwartz, and also by his dental records.

But the fire chief was suspicious, thinking that the fire had been deliberately started, possibly after the man whose body was found had been killed. When Schwartz's wife was informed of this she suggested that her husband might have been murdered by someone trying to obtain his secret formula. The police then discovered that there had been a travelling missionary, Gilbert Barbe, in the area, who now had disappeared.

The local sheriff decided to call in Dr Heinrich, a professor at the University of California at San Francisco and a noted criminologist. He made a careful examination of the site of the fire and also examined the charred corpse. He came to the surprising conclusion that the body was not that of Charles Schwartz. Although efforts had been made to make it look like the inventor's, even to the extent of removing some teeth so that the dental pattern corresponded, a photograph of Schwartz showed that his ear lobes were a different shape to those of the corpse.

Dr Heinrich also found evidence that the body had been stored in a cupboard before being burned. Thus it could not have been Schwartz because he was known to have phoned home just before the explosion. Plainly the inventor had made elaborate plans to disappear, including taking out a $200,000 insurance policy on his life, and had murdered Barbe to take his place. Dr Heinrich also found that the chemical factory where Schwartz was apparently conducting experiments to manufacture a substitute for silk was also a fraud, set up no doubt to dupe businessmen into putting money into the scheme. There wasn't even water or gas laid on in the building.

The police believed that Mrs Schwartz was a party to the scam and by watching her they eventually traced Schwartz to a boarding house in Oakland. But he shot himself just as the police were breaking down the door to get in.

References
Son of Sam
Son of Sam by L. D. Klausner, McGraw-Hill, 1981

Peter Kurten
Monsters of Weimar by Theodor Lessing, Mo Croasdale, Nemesis Books, 1993

Charles Schwartz
The Limits of Detection by Douglas Wynn, Warner Books, 1992
The Chemist of Crime by Eugene B. Block, Cassell, 1959

Drugs

Drug dealing is estimated to be the biggest illegal economic activity in the UK today, far outstripping the money involved in stolen goods, prostitution and massage parlours. Although the domestic production of cannabis is said to be on a large scale, the vast majority of illegal drugs consumed in this country comes from overseas. It is estimated that customs seize perhaps 20 per cent, but that still leaves a very large amount smuggled into Britain every year.

Before the use of sniffer dogs, smugglers would pack drugs into suitcases, but contraband like this is easily picked up by the sensitive noses of the dogs. Then smugglers began carrying quantities of drugs strapped to their bodies under their clothes. People who do this are often known as 'mules' and they are much less likely to be detected by sniffer dogs. A further development is the use of 'stuffers' and 'swallowers', as they are called, who conceal drugs, usually wrapped in plastic packets, actually inside their bodies. Many of these are women.

A tragic case occurred in the early 1980s. Ian Fuller was a 22-year-old barman who was working in London when he was approached by an Asian businessman. The man asked Fuller if he would be prepared to smuggle two video recorders and some video tapes into India. He said that Fuller would be approached at Delhi airport by a customs official who had been bribed to pass him through without a search and that in return Fuller would be given a fortnight's 'all expenses paid' holiday in India for him and his girl-friend.

Fuller readily agreed, but when they arrived at Delhi airport there was no sign of a corrupt offical and their luggage was searched. The videos were found and he was asked to pay 300 per cent on the value as import duty. He refused and left the equipment at the airport. But it seemed to make no difference to the Asian businessman and his associates, who met the couple outside the airport as agreed. And the holiday went ahead as promised. In fact it was extended by an extra couple of weeks. But Fuller's girlfriend found that he was a bit quiet in the latter half of their holiday and seemed to be having frequent conversations with the Asian businessman, while she was left alone in their hotel room.

They returned to England in September and to the flat in London Fuller shared with a friend. Fuller said that he was not feeling well and retired to bed. Later that night the friend was roused by shouts from Fuller's girlfriend and going into their room found that he was having convulsions. They called the ambulance service, but the barman died before he reached hospital. The autopsy showed that he had swallowed 367 capsules of heroin, each one being sealed in rubber, either from the ends of condoms or the fingers of rubber gloves. But eight of them had burst open and Fuller had died from acute heroin poisoning.

Fuller's girlfriend said that he had told her before he died that during the holiday he had been approached and asked to act as a mule. It had been suggested to him that both he and his girlfriend could bring back equal quantities by swallowing capsules. But he, to spare his girlfriend, had agreed to swallow the whole quantity himself – with tragic consequences.

References
Real-Life Crimes, vol.2, Part 17, Eaglemoss Publications Ltd., 1993
The Times
The Sunday Times

Fraud

Fraud is said to be the world's fastest growing industry. It costs UK companies something like £5 billion every year. Crimes may range from insider trading on the stock market, art forgery, maritime fraud (deliberately sinking ships to claim the insurance) video pirating, to computer hacking (which can involve in part obtaining illegal access to bank funds and diverting them to the hacker's account). The ways that the criminals are tracked down and brought to justice make fascinating reading and will suggest many plots for crime writers. But a story with a slightly more human angle is the Barlow Clewes affair.

When Leslie and Emmy Mullard returned from holiday in the summer of 1988 they heard that a Barlow Clewes company had gone into receivership. They themselves had invested over £60,000, the whole of their life savings, and now it had disappeared. And since they lived in retirement on the returns from their investments, so had their income. They had to sell their home to make enough to live on. And theirs was the story of thousands of other small investors who had lost money with the company.

Peter Clowes was and is a brilliant man. Born in Manchester, he left school at fifteen to work in his parents' hardware shop. But his facility with figures soon pushed him into selling insurance and he was so successful that in 1973 he went into partnership with Elizabeth Barlow to form the Barlow Clewes investment company. Elizabeth Barlow left the partnership in 1978, but the company continued to prosper and by the early 1980s Clowes was in control of two companies, Barlow Clewes Gilt Managers and Barlow Clewes International, which was based in Gibraltar. Both apparently invested solely in gilts, which are UK government bonds with a fixed rate of interest, and are attractive to cautious investors.

In the early 1980s Clowes began a process known as 'bond washing', which is essentially buying gilts just after they have paid out their half yearly dividend, when they are supposed to be at their lowest price, and selling just before the payout of the next dividend, when they are at their highest. This apparently enabled him to offer a better return on investments than his competitors and this, combined with heavy promotion, attracted a lot of money. By 1985 he was handling in excess of £100 million of investors' funds. But what the public did not know was that the bond washing had benefited him very little and the increased interest percentages over his competitors had been obtained by paying old investors with new investors' money. And in addition he was siphoning off funds from his companies to sustain a millionaire's life style. He bought a large chateau in France, two private jets and a luxury ocean-going yacht.

The government banned bond washing early in 1985 and it looked as if Clowes's advantage had disappeared, but he continued to promote his companies heavily and paid so-called independent financial advisers to recommend his companies. Money continued to flood in.

The Department of Trade and Industry (DTI) had begun investigating the Barlow Clowes companies in 1983 when it was realised he was trading without a licence. In March 1985 it announced that his accounting records were not up to requirements, but the civil servants looking into the situation were of the opinion that Barlow Clowes was a basically sound and honest business and in October he was given a licence to continue trading. It was to be a very costly mistake.

It was two years later when Barlow Clowes's accountants reported that the company's records hadn't improved and the Bank of England wrote to the DTI saying they were worried about the Barlow Clowes operation. But it took another eight months before the Securities and Investments Board (SIB), the City's most senior regulator, asked the Offical Receiver to put Barlow Clowes Gilt Managers, one of the subsidiaries, into provisional liquidation. Subsequently a number of documents were lodged with the High Court alleging falsification of documents. There seemed to be £139 million missing.

To the mostly pensioner investors it looked as if they were not going to get their money back, but to the SIB it seemed as if a certain amount of criminality was involved and the Serious Fraud Office – only founded in April 1988 to detect and prosecute serious financial crimes – was called in. Peter Clowes was arrested at his Poynton,

Cheshire, home and he and three former colleagues were tried in London in July 1991. The trial lasted until February 1992, when Clowes was convicted of ten theft and eight fraud charges. His second-in-command was convicted of one theft charge and the other two men were acquitted. Clowes was sentenced to ten years' imprisonment, although he served only four.

There was a happier ending for the investors. Because the DTI had initially investigated and taken no action against Barlow Clowes, indeed had allowed him to go on trading, the Parliamentary Ombudsman concluded that the department had been guilty of significant maladministration. Although the DTI never accepted the findings it did make an *ex gratia* payment of £150 million to the investors who had lost money.

References
Fraudbusters by Mark Killick, Victor Gollancz, 1998
Profits of Deceit by Patricia Franklin, William Heinemann, 1990
The Daily Telegraph
The Sunday Times

Piracy

Most people think of piracy, which is defined as an armed attack on ships at sea, as the Spanish Main, doubloons and pieces of eight, and old Hollywood films; but unfortunately it is very much alive today. There are more than 100 cases of piracy reported every year, from the robbing of tourists on hired yachts around the coast of Albania, for example, to the full-scale hijacking of cargo vessels.

An interesting case was reported recently in the *Criminologist* magazine. On September 12th 1995 the *Anna Sierra*, carrying a cargo of bags of sugar, was boarded by pirates off the coast near the borders of Thailand and Cambodia. This usually takes place by the thieves arriving in a high-speed launch late at night, throwing a grapnel aboard the vessel and then climbing up the rope. The gang which took over the cargo ship was thirty-strong and armed with automatic weapons. The crew of twenty-two and the Greek master were hand-cuffed in pairs and locked up for two days. Then eight of the crew were set adrift, on a rickety home-made raft of oil drums and planks of wood, in the shark-infested sea. They were soon thrown into the water by the waves, but they clung to the wreckage for three hours before being rescued by some Vietnamese fishermen. The rest of the crew were made to board a life raft and driven off by gunfire. But they too were lucky and were picked up by fishing boats and taken ashore.

When the master was able, he got in touch with the ship's owners and an international search was instituted for the missing vessel. The International Maritime Bureau posted notices to 800 harbour masters together with a photograph of the vessel and a substantial reward was offered. After ten days a shipping agency in China was paid $50,000 after reporting seeing the vessel in Behai, South China. The harbour master there had become suspicious when the vessel, now called *Arct*ic, had arrived unexpectedly at the port, and the crew's docu-ments proved to be forged. The vessel and its cargo were impounded and the crew not allowed to leave the ship. Two years later the slow process of Chinese law had still not allowed the vessel and its cargo to be released to the owners and the hijackers, after being held ashore for several months, were eventually released without charge.

An intriguing mystery with a flavour of piracy occurred on the tiny remote atoll of Palmyra in the middle of the Pacific Ocean, 1000 miles due south of Hawaii, in September 1974, and was recounted in the book *And the Sea Will Tell*. Two yachts were tied up near each other in the lagoon of the atoll. One, the *Sea Wind*, was a well equipped and well maintained sea-going yacht owned by Eleanor (known as Muff) and her husband Malcolm Graham, a 43-year-old engineer from San Diego. The other was the *Iola*, not such a sturdy or desirable vessel, the property of Buck Walker and his girlfriend Jennifer Jenkins. Walker was a 36-year-old Californian who had been in prison for armed robbery and dealing in drugs, and was wanted by the federal authorities on a drugs charge.

About this time radio contact with the Grahams ceased and later

Walker and his girlfriend were seen in Hawaii with the *Sea Wind*. But it was to be another seven years before a young woman found some bones on the island of Palmyra that were later identified as being part of Muff Graham's skeleton. Malcolm's remains have never been discovered. Buck Walker was convicted of the murder of Eleanor Graham in February 1986, while Jennifer Jenkins was acquitted.

References
The Criminologist,vol. 22, no. 1, 1998
Piracy Today by Captain Roger Villar, Conway Maritime Press, 1985
And the Sea Will Tell by Vincent Bugliosi with Bruce B. Henderson, W. W. Norton & Co., 1991

Robbery

Small-scale robberies, from shops or houses, occasionally lead to murder if the perpetrator is cornered and resorts to violence to escape and this type of case is covered in another section of the book. Large-scale robberies are much less common, but their planning, execution and the eventual discovery of the criminals make interesting and exciting stories. The fact that large-scale robberies are usually committed by a team of criminals also allows for character development in stories based on the crimes, and the inevitable clash between the personalities makes for conflict, the cornerstone of most fiction.

Among the more famous are the robbery at the North Terminal Garage in Boston, US, in 1950 (known as the Brinks robbery), the English Great Train Robbery of 1966, the bank raid on the Société Generale in Nice in 1976 and the Brinks-Mat robbery near Heathrow in 1983. All except the Nice robbery have had very successful films made from the stories, but space permits me to describe only one.

The Brinks-Mat security building occupied a site on an industrial estate near Heathrow Airport. It was really a series of large safes used to hold valuable cargo, like bullion, bank notes and jewellery being transported to or from the airports around London. On Saturday,

November 26th 1983, of the cargoes held one was gold bars for shipment to the Far East. At 6.40 in the morning five men hidden by balaclavas and carrying automatic pistols and shotguns entered the building and surprised the six guards. The guards were tied up and blindfolded. Their trousers were torn open and petrol poured on their genitals. They were then threatened that if they did not reveal the combinations of the various safes they would be set alight or mutilated with knives. The terrified guards readily complied. Indeed one man was so frightened that he could not remember his part of the security combination.

But the robbers had enough to get into the vaults, where they found shoebox-sized parcels of gold bars. They loaded these into two lorries and drove off. The robbers were themselves surprised at the amount they had got away with. They had taken 6800 bars, valued then at £26 million. It was the biggest robbery there had ever been in this country.

The Flying Squad was notified and the commanding officer took personal charge of the investigations. The obvious thing was to examine the backgrounds of each of the security guards to see if there was a chance it was an 'inside job'. One of the guards, Anthony Black, was found to be the brother-in-law of a well known villain, Brian Robinson. After intensive questioning Black finally confessed and named Robinson and Michael McAvoy and another man as being involved in the robbery. He also said that he had made impressions of keys to the outside doors of the security unit and had given information on safe combinations and security routines.

Black received six years for his part in the robbery and was the star witness in the subsequent trials of the others. Robinson and McAvoy received twenty-five years each, but the other man was acquitted because of the lack of evidence against him.

But that wasn't the end of the story. The gang had £26 million in gold bullion to dispose of. They decided to melt it down, mix it with base metals to disguise its high purity and sell it on the open market as 'scrap gold'. One man the police suspected of being involved was Kenneth Noye and his large house and extensive grounds in West

Kingsdown, Kent was put under a 24-hour watch. Unfortunately one of the surveillance team was surprised in the grounds by Noye's three Rottweiler dogs. Noye came out of the house and during the confrontation the policeman was stabbed several times and died before reaching hospital.

Noye was charged with murder, but acquitted on the grounds of self-defence. The incident however sparked off a concerted effort by Scotland Yard against the suspects and at least a dozen were convicted and received sentences of up to fourteen years, although only a very small amount of the stolen gold was recovered.

References

The Nice Robbery
The Sewers of Gold by Albert Spaggiari, Granada, 1979

The Great Train Robbery
The Train Robbers by Piers Paul Read, W. H. Allen, 1978

The Brinks-Mat Robbery
The Flying Squad by Neil Darbyshire and Brian Hilliard, Headline, 1993
Public Enemy Number 1 by Wensley Clarkson, Blake, 1997

BIBLIOGRAPHY
Books and Magazines on True Crime

Booksellers who Specialise in 'True Crime' Books

Clifford Elmer Books, 8 Balmoral Avenue, Cheadle Hulme, Cheadle, Cheshire SK8 5EQ. Tel: 0161 485 7064 Fax: 0161 485 7068
e-mail: TrueCrime@compuserve.com or CliffBooks@aol.com

Grey House Books, 60 Portobello Road, London W11 3DL Tel: 020 7221 0269

Crime In Store, 14 Bedford Street, Covent Garden, London WC2E 9HE. Tel: 020 7379 3795 Fax: 020 7379 8988
e-mail: CrimeBks@aol.com
Website: htttp://nt.pleasuredomes.co.uk/crimeinstore.html

murder one, 71–73 Charing Cross Road, London WC2H 0AA. Tel: 020 7734 3483 Fax: 020 7734 3429
e-mail: 106562.2021@compuserve.com
Website: www.murderone.co.uk

Encyclopedia-type Books

The New Murderers Who's Who by J. H. H. Gaute and Robin Odell, Harrap, 1989
World Encyclopedia of 20th Century Murder by Jay Robert Nash, Headline, 1992
The New Encyclopedia of Serial Killers by Brian Lane and Wilfred Gregg, Headline, 1996

Books Containing Smaller Numbers of Cases

Themed

Settings for Slaughter by Douglas Wynn, Robert Hale, 1988 (thirteen cases where the location of the murder played an important part in the story)

Medical Murders by Jonathan Goodman, Piatkus, 1991 (thirteen true tales of murder associated with the medical profession)

For Love of Money by Georgina Lloyd, Robert Hale, 1991 (sixteen murders for gain)

Paid to Kill by Frank Jones, Headline, 1995 (twelve true stories of hit men)

Geographical

Murders and Mysteries from the North York Moors by Peter N. Walker, Robert Hale, 1988

Murder Casebook – Cheshire by Steve Fielding, Countryside Books, 1996

Murderous Derbyshire by John J. Eddleston, Breedon Books, 1997

'Rough Justice' Types

A Reasonable Doubt by Julian Symons, The Cresset Press, 1960

Rough Justice by Martin Young and Peter Hill, Ariel Books, 1983

Miscarriages of Justice by Bob Woffinden, Hodder & Stoughton, 1987

Forensic Science

Murder under the Microscope by Philip Paul, Macdonald, 1990

Forensic Fingerprints by Hugh Miller, Headline, 1998

Crimebusting by Jenny Ward, Blandford, 1998

One Case per Book

'Rough justice' Types

The Airman and the Carpenter by Ludovic Kennedy, Viking, 1985

Murder at the Farm by Paul Foot, Sidgwick & Jackson, 1986

Innocents by Jonathan Rose with Steve Panter and Trevor Wilkinson, Fourth Estate, 1997

British and European

Easing the Passing by Patrick Devlin, The Bodley Head, 1985

The Camden Town Murder by Sir David Napley, Weidenfeld and Nicolson, 1987

The Peasenhall Murder by Martin Fido & Keith Skinner, Alan Sutton, 1990

Little Gregory by Charles Penwarden, Fourth Estate, 1990

A Question of Evidence by Christopher Berry-Dee with Robin Odell, W. H. Allen, 1991

American

The Stranger beside Me by Ann Rule, New American Library, 1996

From Cradle to Grave by Joyce Egginton, William Morrow and Co., Inc. (BCA), 1989

Poisoned Blood by Philip E. Ginsburg, Michael O'Mara, 1992

Lethal Lolita by Maria Eftimiades, Michael O'Mara, 1992

Biographies, Memoirs

Police

Detective Days by Frederick Porter Wensley, Cassell, 1931

Occupied with Crime by Sir Richard Jackson, Harrap, 1967

Believe No One by Roy Herridge with Brian Hilliard, Little, Brown, 1993

Lawyers

The Life of Marshall Hall by Edward Marjoribanks MP, Gollancz, 1936

Sir Travers Humphreys by Douglas G. Browne, Harrap, 1960

Norman Birkett by H. Montgomery Hyde, Hamish Hamilton, 1964

Forensic Scientists

The Chemist of Crime by Eugene B. Block, Cassell, 1959

Expert Witness by H. J. Walls, John Long, 1972

Crime Scientist by John Thompson, W. H. Allen, 1982

Forensic Pathologists

Mostly Murder by Sir Sidney Smith, Harrap, 1959

Forty Years of Murder by Professor Keith Simpson, Harrap, 1978

Dr Ian West's Casebook by Chester Stern, Warner Books, 1997

Forensic Psychiatrists and Psychologists

Criminal Shadows by David Canter, HarperCollins, 1994

The Jigsaw Man by Paul Britton, Bantam Press, 1997

FBI

Whoever Fights Monsters by Robert K. Ressler, Simon & Schuster, 1992

Mindhunter by John Douglas and Mark Olshaker, Heinemann, 1996

Books on Trials

Single Case Books

'Notable British Trials' series (eighty-three titles), William Hodge & Co. Ltd.

'Famous Trials' series (sixteen titles), Penguin Books

'Old Bailey Trials' series (seven titles), Jarrolds

'Celebrated Trials' series (six titles), David & Charles

Books Containing Collections of Trials

Famous American Trials by C. E. Bechhofer Roberts, Jarrolds, 1947

Famous Trials by The First Earl of Birkenhead, Hutchinson & Co.

More Famous Trials by The First Earl of Birkenhead, Hutchinson & Co.

A Book of Trials by Sir Travers Humphreys, Heinemann, 1953

Magazines Publishing True Crime

Master Detective, True Detective, True Crime Detective Monthly (all published monthly by Forum Press, P.O. Box 158, London SE20 7QA)

Murder Most Foul (published quarterly by Forum Press)

Murder in Mind (a Marshall Cavendish Reference Collection, issues published every two weeks)

Overseas magazines available in this country

Detective Cases, Detective Dragnet, Detective Files, Headquarters Detective, Startling Detective, True Police (all published twice monthly by Globe Communications Corp, 1350 Sherbrooke Street West, Suite 600, Montreal, Quebec H3G 2T4, Canada)

Official Detective (published by Offical Detective, P.O. Box 53393, Boulder, Colorado 80322-3393, USA)